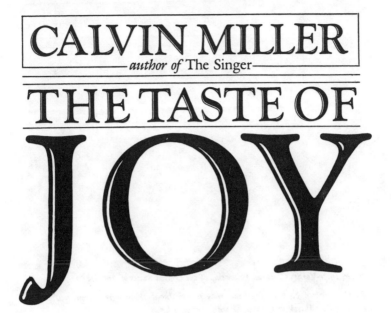

CALVIN MILLER
author of The Singer

THE TASTE OF
JOY

INTER-VARSITY PRESS
DOWNERS GROVE
ILLINOIS 60515

InterVarsity Press is the book-publishing division of Inter-Varsity Christian Fellowship, a student movement active on campus at hundreds of universities, colleges and schools of nursing. For information about local and regional activities, write IVCF, 233 Langdon St., Madison, WI 53703.

Portions of this book first appeared in That Elusive Thing Called Joy © 1975 by Calvin Miller.

Distributed in Canada through InterVarsity Press, 860 Denison St., Unit 3, Markham, Ontario L3R 4H1, Canada.

All Scripture quotations, unless otherwise indicated, are from the Revised Standard Version of the Bible, copyrighted 1946, 1952, © 1971, 1973.

Cover photograph: Robert McKendrick

ISBN 0-87784-831-9

Printed in the United States of America

Library of Congress Cataloging in Publication Data
Miller, Calvin.
   The taste of joy.

   Includes bibliographical references.
   1. Christian life—Baptist authors.   I. Title.
BV4501.2.M4727   1983   248.4'861   83-7839
ISBN 0-87784-831-9

17   16   15   14   13   12   11   10   9   8   7   6   5   4   3   2   1
95   94   93   92   91   90   89   88   87   86   85   84   83

We are afraid to accept what is given to us; we are in compulsive self-seclusion toward our world. We try to escape life instead of controlling it.
Paul Tillich, **The New Being**

The mind is its own place, and in itself Can make a Heav'n of Hell, a Hell of Heav'n.
John Milton

Love is . . . a free gift. . . . And it is most itself, most free, when it is offered in spite of suffering, of injustice, and of death.
Archibald MacLeish

I
Happiness—
Mind
over
Mood

MILLIONS OF CHRISTIANS are miserable and surprised at their misery. They were promised joy and bliss if only they would "receive Christ." Eagerly they did so, and were astounded that the life they came to know in Christ was as dyspeptic in many ways as the life they left on the other side of repentance. Somewhere in their initial depression they felt cheated, for the Christ-life was yet filled with hunger and inner struggle. Their disenchantment seemed unbearable. Drawn to Christ by the magnetism of his well-being, they found themselves in a chronic, futile search for a happiness greater than that of those who preceded them in faith.

For the first few hours after their conversion, they were indeed happy. Then the warmth cooled and later died! Close upon the flush of the warm mood, the cold realization came. Had they merely created the feeling themselves? Had they just trumped up a mindset that could not endure the stress they had to face? Was Christ anemic or did the problem lie within themselves? Did they need a new retreat into longer prayers or more furious Bible study? They were obsessed with how to recover the lost glow of their first love for Christ.

Their struggle was not entirely futile. They did recover a little joy here and there—an inspirational church service or an unexpected quiet talk with a Christian who seemed happy in spite of Christianity. But these "happiness" flashes were usually short-lived. Again and again their lives became an anxious search for contentment. With feelings of emptiness, some dropped out of church. Others pushed themselves into recruiting new converts in a sustained desire to make themselves believe. "Let Jesus come into your heart and you will be happy!" In their shallow evangelism they but advanced the error.

I began my own walk with Christ surrounded by such easy and "churchy" slogans of joy. I attended a revival service where both Jesus and joy came into my life. For years I lived beneath the great delusion that the two were the same. Inwardly I believed that Christ and joy could not be one. I felt the presence of Christ from time to time, but all too often I was a peaceless and ulcerated disciple.

Christ kept his word, "Lo, I am with you always." Gradually, I came to see that Christ was always there and yet happiness was not. Happiness, like a fickle friend, flitted in and out of my moody and unpredictable spasms of religiosity. What a set of ups and downs came in with Jesus! Never did happiness leave me but his ugly alter ego, depression, moved in with leaden boots to keep my feet from any dance.

Many Christians confuse happiness with joy, as did I. Happiness is a buoyant emotion that results from the momentary plateaus of well-being that characterize our lives. Joy is bedrock stuff, on the other hand. Joy is a confidence that operates irrespective of our moods. Joy is the certainty that all is well, however we feel.

My infantile Christianity became a struggle to find happiness in the world around me. Everyone was seeking happiness inside and outside the church. The secular world was hungry for it too. In my childhood the "somebody" sisters had sung the intriguing invitation, "Forget your troubles; come on, get happy!" This song also bore the surface truth that if you can forget your troubles, you will quite likely "get happy." But the song was based on the fallacy that people can generate happiness as an act of will. I could see what those without Christ could not: that self-generated contentment is spastic and punctuated by hangovers of insecurity and despair. Joy is not a matter of simple will or all the world would have it.

Insecurity and despair are widespread afflictions in these years when Western culture itself seems unsure of its future. The usual way of coping with our fears of the future is to ignore them. To stick one's head in the sand, however, does not work for long. Ignoring life may shut out our desperation, but it does not fill our need for purpose and meaning. Reluctantly or willingly we are always propelled into the real, harsh world. We all feel trapped in a society where there is no exit from our despondency.

The Focus of Faith
Faith offers us a new focus. We come to see that there is another, unseen reality where meaning exists in abundance. Through faith we discover the Christ-dimension and are released from our slavery to the here and now. With faith, however, we can return to our hurried lives as renewed people, for we have touched a plane of reality that freed us from captivity to ourselves to belong to something and Someone greater.

Faith flowers in the secret places of our hearts. Here is an inwardness so inward that like the dark side of the moon, it is never to be viewed.

In recent years I have learned the difference between faith and the moody obsession I once thought it to be. I once drove furiously to be happy and in my confusion I called this mad urge the pilgrimage of faith. How slowly I learned that faith is not a hunger to be happy.

So much sour Christianity has resulted from this *happiness drive*. It is often this compulsion which lures the frustrated to Christ for the first time. And the same drive continues in Christians as an insatiable appetite for ever higher and higher plateaus of mood.

The feeling is that if we can only walk harder, love more, pray longer, witness better or visit the elderly more frequently, we will, in time, achieve the breakthrough. There at last, happiness will be gloriously ours, and so utter and lasting that no tyrant or circumstance can wrench it from our lives.

Those who seek happiness too intensely will have little of it. Nothing is more barren than the pursuit of happiness. It is like lemmings driving madly toward the sea. Happiness is not something you press to achieve as you might struggle to bowl a 300 game. Still, this is the way most believers go about it.

The error of pursuing happiness can be seen simply by considering basic definitions. The word *happiness* has the same root as the word *happening*. *Happiness happens*. It is the result of life which is at rest. When our circumstances are warm and comfortable, when our lives are secure, happiness simply occurs. But joy is not a momentary occurrence subject to change with climate or religious motivation. Rather it rises above mood and circumstances and transcends our fickle moments of elation.

Perhaps the notion that we can trump up a state of joy comes from the evangelistic services we have attended. The image yet chills me; I have sat in worship services singing that my heart was full of joy when I was not sure that I was ever going to be able to handle life as it had been given to me to live. Even as I sang, I looked about to wonder if we were not all trying to smile and sing ourselves into a condition we said we had.

If we were prone to sing too softly of this elusive joy, a boisterous Christian urged us to "really smile and turn around and shake hands" with the happy people behind us. Such odd combinations of positive-thinking group dynamics only widened the chasm in our lives. We dared not stop singing or we would have wept.

Joy: All around Us

The pursuit of loud singing and forced smiling can be shattered easily. It is a kind of pep-rally-and-bonfire answer to emptiness. Joy is more than cheering oneself in worship. Joy, like life, is all about us. We cannot pursue what already accompanies us and, indeed, surrounds us.

Looking for happiness is like looking for the boundary marker that separates states or countries. The lines are invisible to the naked eye. I once drove my family through the borderlands of Austria and Germany. It was often impossible to tell whether we were in one country or the other because of the serpentine roads. I often discovered that I was completely surrounded by the beauty of Austria and yet under the absurd impression that I wanted to be there.

Joy in Christ knows no markers that read, "Joy Begins Here!" We were born in Christ and thus come to be in the very bosom of the Almighty. We are always in God! The Scriptures teach that in him we live and move and have our being.

To discover God is merely to open the heart and to admit that he, for whom we have searched, is overwhelmingly about us—indeed, invading our very being with joy. He engulfs us as pure love because we have quit pushing and have become willing to wait for his coming.

It is God's nearness that makes him invisible. Inwardness is sometimes the last place we seek him and the only place he can be found. Near as God is, we still foolishly hurry outward: we lift our seeking eyes as if to find him in the obscure distance. Like sailors on submarine duty, we move through the ocean with the periscope up to search the surface world. How slowly we learn that life is not upon the sea but within it! Beneath the water those who seek with us urgently insist—"What do you see?"

"Nothing!" answers the fellow struggler, straining to see through the ocular of the scope.

But his is a dishonest report. He does see something. He sees miles and miles of water. There is so much water that he is prone to discount it altogether.

"In him we live and move and have our being." God's greatness was where we found eternal life, and in his vastness we must live it out. When we move through him, if we dare to travel "up periscope," all that shall meet our vision is his universal presence. Like the crew of a submarine, we must honor the presence all about us. Submerged in him, we dare not open even the tiniest hatch in our lives or our whole world view will be flooded with his abundance.

It goes without saying that where there is so much of God and joy about us, we shall never know much about them without a new way of seeing what, indeed, is close at hand. Again we do not have to go anywhere to find joy; we only have to be open to God. Too long we have gone seeking happiness in a vain pilgrimage; now we must throw open the windows of our closed being and train our focus not outward toward some mountain retreat, but inward toward the near God who already dwells there in fullness.

Joy, likewise, is a matter of peace regardless of circumstances. St. Paul testified that he had learned contentment in every state in which he found himself. John the Baptist reminded Caesar's soldiers that there was a simple splendor in being content with their wages. Our prayer should not be "Lord, make me happy," but, "This moment is enough. I will not try to wring it for an extra drop of nectar."

Our minds sin against the present. It is lovely enough as it is. We must not force it to yield more joy because our minds are malcontent. What treachery our unhappy egos work! They will not be satisfied with any circumstance. "Why is this rose only this sweet? There must be one sweeter, buried deeper in the thorns." "A bigger house would be better, surely." Such emotional avarice keeps us reaching with our sensors exposed like "feeling addicts"! We want to feel all we can. We move from sensuous experience to sensuous experience, seeking the higher highs that our gluttonous nervous system denied to us by ignoring the adequate and lovely present.

Joy: The Result, Not the Goal

This damnable lust to titillate not only makes us miserable with what we have, it causes us to indict Christian worship. We condemn preaching as drab and gray when we compare it to the rainbows of drama and art and music we find elsewhere. The strobe and stereo impact of a rock concert interlaced with the sweetness of marijuana haze are evidence that we want to put all the "feel" we can into feeling. This tendency in less extreme forms causes us to walk out of church disgusted because Christian truth in a hyped-up world seems so bland.

Of course the show must get better week by week since we cannot be content with things as they are. Perhaps the greatest weakness of the charismatic movement is this unfortunate yen to titillate the sensors of Christians by seeking to put more fireworks in their faith. Such Christians often burn out on high-voltage worship and are left disconsolate over the powerful but simple truth which first marked their entrance to faith. This glandular approach to joy assumes that God exists in his fullness to make Christians feel good.

Church, however, does not exist to make us happy. Yet so often we hear, "I don't feel happy when I leave this church," or, "Don't you think you should feel good when you leave church?" Of course, no one wants to attend a church which offers little spontaneity or joy. While happiness may result from worship, joy is not the goal of great worship. Indeed it may precede it.

Neither does God exist to make us happy. Anyone who holds such a preposterous view is going to have a miserable relationship with God. He does not lavish his children with a jolly discipleship so that they may swim in spiritual ecstasy between conversion and death. God is a giver, but he does not give happiness. He gives redemption, meaning, security, love, victory and the indwelling of the Holy Spirit. And happiness is our response to his gifts.

We do not become joyous and say, "Let's pray," but after prayer we may find ourselves in touch with a deeper joy. Rarely does joy result in reading God's Word, but reading the Bible can nourish our joy, which is the result of spiritual discipline.

This is true also in the arts or in sports. The concert artist finds delight in her talent only if she has been thoroughly disciplined in practice. Then following her third curtain call, a great glow fills her life. In the excitement of victory the quarterback is scooped up to ride on the shoulders of his teammates. Yet his spontaneous enthusiasm comes only from the discipline which preceded it. The football team did not go to the game trying to be happy and rehearsing how they would tear down the goal posts.

As ridiculous as this sounds for the football team, this is precisely how a great many Christians are living. We live in search of an emotional high. Faith we feel is God's gift to the nervous system. We go to church seeking feeling. Often we have had little or no spiritual discipline. Frustration and despair set in. We go to worship with our emotional antennae exposed to receive the excitement of the group. But such feelings are seldom fruitful or permanent.

Philippians 2:12 asks us as Christians to "work out your own salvation with fear and trembling." This "work out" does not mean that God asks us to save ourselves; it means that everything we receive at salvation we receive in embryo. We must apply discipline to our infant gifts. All believers are potentially great and happy Christians. Our happiness is ruined by our neglect of the discipline principle.

Neglect is the opposite of discipline. Suppose you have been given a large portion of fertile ground. However, it is covered with timber, boulders and debris. Now the happiness you derive from that property will be in direct proportion to what it produces. And what it produces will be in direct proportion to the neglect or discipline you give it. If you clear the timber and debris—though it takes much effort—you will be pleased with the product. If you neglect your gift, it will never produce anything, and your life will be as miserable after a while as if you had received no gift at all.

Three things I do every morning so I will be happy all day long. The first is to affirm the reality of Jesus Christ and to thank him for his lordship. The second is to call to mind the reality of Satan, who will seek throughout the day to make me a miserable contradiction of evident joy. Third, I call to mind the gifts that are mine in Christ. If I live each day faithful to my gifts, developing and improving them, I find I am, indeed, a happy person. If I am sloppy and careless in developing my gifts, I find a predictable negativity fixing itself into my life.

Joy: The Centrality of Study
Consider the relationship of the word *discipline* to the word

disciple. A key idea in the word *disciple* is that of pupil. Thus the chief discipline of the disciple is study, acquiring knowledge through learning. To be a *disciple* is to be under *discipline*.

Many disciples would like the happiness that comes from discipline, but they also want to avoid the hard work. Millions of us believers do not take our Christianity seriously simply because discipleship is rigorous and tiring. We drift from service to service, studying only enough to keep a little self-respect with our peers. We have misinterpreted *disciple* to mean "convert."

No lazy student ever felt good on report-card day. But countless serious students feel great when they receive good marks because they have been industrious.

Never have there been so many disciples who did so little studying. Yet in our age the proliferation of Christian resources for study is astounding. Books are everywhere. It is only in recent history that we have had such time and resources. In spite of this, our day is plagued by hordes of miserable Christians whose pitiful study habits give them few victories and much frustration. Serious students will develop dynamic minds and a confident use of the gifts God has given to them.

Consistent joy is mind-first rather than mood-first. While everyone likes to be in a good mood, it is treacherous to try to build anything stable for Christ solely on the basis of our moods.

The concept of study as the basis for meaning and happiness came primarily out of the Hebrew faith, from which Christianity grew. Most of us view the church as an "experience center," where believers seek to "feel" together in their pilgrimages. The preference for worship over Sunday school among most adults demonstrates this. The synagogue, on the other hand, has traditionally been a "learning center," or a school where study and maturity are emphasized.

The real hub of Jewish religious education is found in the great *shema* of the book of Deuteronomy (6:4). Its essence is, "Hear, O Israel, the Lord our God is one Lord!" And this essential understanding of God was a matter for home education. They were to teach their children these truths in every aspect of daily life.

Let it be remembered that Christ himself was a Jew, and the Jewish people believed (and still do) that happiness and adjustment follow meditation and study. As the Lord promised to Joshua, "This book of the law shall not depart out of your mouth, but you shall meditate on it day and night, that you may be careful to do according to all that is written in it; *for then* you shall make your way prosperous, and then you shall have good success" (Josh 1:8). The rabbi is viewed as the teacher and an authority, and the synagogue is still seen as a classroom.

Conversely, consider Christianity. Many adults know little about the Bible. The preacher is not thought of as a teacher but as a devotionalist. His job is not to educate but to "inspire." Sermons are constructed more often to elicit some emotional response than to stimulate thought. In some churches logic seems to cease completely.

If this judgment seems harsh, one has merely to probe the surface to demonstrate its truth. Any one of the recent questionnaires given to church members indicates that among those who attend regularly there is widespread ignorance of Scripture. In one such poll, many could not name four of the apostles, and few could quote more than one verse from the New Testament. Some even thought "epistles were the wives of apostles."

The title of a Christian folk musical may be an indictment against us—*Natural High*. The implication is that Jesus is the "trip of a lifetime." And that the emotional plateau we can reach with Jesus is greater than one with cocaine.

Many Christians are only "Christaholics" and not disciples at all. Disciples are cross-bearers; they seek Christ. Christaholics seek happiness. Disciples dare to discipline themselves, and the demands they place on themselves leave them enjoying the happiness of their growth. Christaholics are escapists looking for a shortcut to nirvana. Like drug addicts, they are trying to "bomb out" of their depressing world.

There is no automatic joy. Christ is not a happiness capsule; he is the way to the Father. But the way to the Father is not a carnival ride in which we sit and do nothing while we are whisked through various spiritual sensations.

Yet this kind of thinking characterizes a great segment of modern Christianity. It is especially true of youth. Frequently their walk with Christ has not graduated beyond a set of emotional swings. The "Jesus-highs" come between the "human-lows." Many young people have come to believe that such is the natural course of things.

The truth of this judgment is stinging. A roller coaster of spiritual happiness and depression is not what God intends. He wishes for us a consistent growth, unmarked by sporadic emotionalism. The admonition to Timothy is not "*feel* to show thyself approved," but "*study* to show thyself approved" (2 Tim 2:15 KJV).

Of course, the reason for the popularity of inspiration over study is obvious. The devotional is easier than the intellectual. In the book of Exodus, when the children of Israel are delivered from Egypt, they rejoice over the salvation God has provided. Miriam and the women of Israel play tambourines and sing, "The horse and his rider he has thrown into the sea" (Ex 15:21). And while the emotionalism comes easily, a few days later in spiritual despair they are asking, "Is the LORD among us or not?" (Ex 17:7).

The tambourine, however, is a gypsy instrument; it was

most often played by those who had no direction and wandered aimlessly all their lives. Their moods were often electric but seldom consistent. The tambourine was not a difficult instrument to play. One need not study at the conservatory to master it.

Moses was less of a spiritual cheerleader than his sister Miriam. It is not recorded that he played the tambourine, but he did write down the books of the Law for the education of the Jewish nation. They used these laws for the next three thousand years. To master the scrolls that Moses produced in Deuteronomy required the discipline of studying alphabet, grammar, logic and culture.

God knew that the tambourine Miriam praised him with was a fickle and moody instrument. So the stability of the nation was founded on the scrolls, bulky and heavy and filled with tedious Hebrew words. But those words, properly appropriated, would bind the nation consistently to God.

Moses knew (and certainly God knew) that it was from an understanding of the Word that genuine inner contentment came. Human feeling considered alone is not a reliable indication of the authenticity of experience. A public marriage ceremony is no more or less valid because the bride and groom feel some particular way; the bride may have a headache; the whole affair may be emotionally deadpan. Rather, the couple is married if they share the words prescribed by law, whatever their feelings may be.

Joy: Delight in God's Law

As disciples we are to be learners in a continuing affair with the Scripture. No one can be called mature who does not continue to learn; neither can disciples be disciples unless they are gathering day by day an increasing use and understanding of the Word of God.

Peter's admonition was to "grow in grace and *knowledge* of our Lord and Savior Jesus Christ" (2 Pet 3:18). Paul warned us that we ought to "destroy arguments and every proud obstacle to the knowledge of God, and take every thought captive to obey Christ" (2 Cor 10:5). The apostle is clear about it: emotionalism alone will not do it. Paul's teaching on orderly worship in 1 Corinthians 14 illustrates that disruptive emotionalism is taboo. He encouraged the Philippians with, "It is my prayer that your love may abound more and more, with *knowledge* and all discernment" (Phil 1:9). And again he said in Philippians 3, "Indeed I count everything as loss because of the surpassing worth of knowing Christ Jesus my Lord" (v. 8).

Again and again the Scriptures teach the importance of study for consistent Christian living. Therefore, happy Christians have no alternative but to learn the Bible. Remember Romans 15:4: "For whatever was written in former days was written for our instruction." Remember also God's caution to Israel in Hosea 4:6: "My people are destroyed for lack of knowledge." The maturity from which happiness ensues is never easily attained. But we will, with each new plateau of understanding, experience a growing appreciation of how God's Word is the matrix from which the most practical kinds of problems find their solutions.

Paul uses an interesting word in connection with study. It is translated "sound" in the King James Version and the Revised Standard Version. But the word actually means "healthy." Here is the substitution in three different contexts. First of all, Paul exhorts us to have a healthy reason: "Follow the pattern of the *healthy* words which you have heard from me (2 Tim 1:13). Then after beginning with healthy reason, we are to seek out *healthy* teaching. "He must hold firm to the sure word as taught, so that he may be able to give instruction in *healthy* doctrine and also to refute those who contradict it" (Tit 1:9).

The implications of this are tremendous: You can be a healthy Christian only if you are seeking healthy reason and healthy teaching. It is difficult to find anyone who is both happy and sick. Confident believers must be students, and out of their studies will issue people who are "*healthy* in the faith" (Tit 1:13).

Paul's objection to the Cretan Christians (Tit 1:10-12) was that they were "slow bellies" or lazy. Lazy disciples may emote or repent or sing lustily all in an attempt to excuse themselves from the arduous life of discipleship. They would do better to goad themselves into diligence and study. Just as Christ promised, his yoke is never heavy and his burden is ever light, so it is foolish to avoid the life of study because it is hard. Study, while demanding, is never grievous. The outcome of learning the Bible is a love for its content and a respect for its relevancy. The Word which comes to dwell in our lives is itself the parent of joy. Remember the great First Psalm? It blessed the man whose delight was in the Law of the Lord, especially if the man meditated upon the Word of the Lord. And notice that happiness and security immediately arise from an inward affair with God's Law.

There is a great principle in constant meditation on Scripture. The mind is a narrow channel, capable of focusing on only one thought at a time. Therefore, if the mind is focusing on the Word of God, it cannot focus on any negative or bothersome issue. This in itself is a sound principle of mental or spiritual health. This health develops as we agree to the discipline of our discipleship.

Joy: No Free Lunch

There is a parable about a king who ordered his wise men to condense all human wisdom into a small and manageable area of print. They returned after twelve years of work with twelve volumes. "It is too large," protested the king, "condense it further!" So the wise men returned in a year and presented one large volume in place of the twelve. "It's still too large," protested the king. They went out again, only to return the following day with a single statement written on a slip of paper—all the world's wisdom in one line: *There is no free lunch.*

While this greatly oversimplifies human wisdom, there does seem to be an inevitable law of cause and effect: We get out of anything just about what we put into it. This book is not to teach that we can ever earn our salvation—we cannot! It is merely to direct us to discover joy in the only place it can be found—the disciplined life. As we study, our lives throb with well-being. As we ignore study, we will, at best, be only miserable or intermittently happy.

Here is incontrovertible truth: Grace is God's gift to us, but discipline is our gift to him... and not to him alone. Discipline is also a rare and vibrant pledge to ourselves. In the consecration of ourselves as living sacrifices, our own study and industry will provide us with a lifetime of rewards, and the gold will be ours.

In the pages which follow I develop eight concepts of discipleship to which joy can become a consistent and confident response. It is my prayer that having studied these, we can rise to a new and joyous plane of living. For every real disciple learns that life in Christ requires a commitment to self-sacrifice out of which faith will indeed be fresh every morning.

*And there is this great light that has appeared in the murk,
like a morning star. It is there, silent and glorious.
An odd road marker. But perhaps a man is asked to go that
way on the supposition that it is not all a ghastly cheat.
Yes. Perhaps that is what is asked.*
Thomas Howard, **Christ the Tiger**

*He is no fool who gives what he cannot keep to gain
what he cannot lose.*
Jim Elliot

All real living is meeting.
Martin Buber

2
Love by Covenant

I CAME TO CHRIST as a child. And in many ways my own first faith was childlike. As a baby cries at the slightest discomfort, so did I in my new life in Christ. I vacillated erratically between need and fulfillment. As an infant requires constant attention, my new life required a lot of maintenance from many people.

This was partly because of the particular teaching of the church I then attended. I was taught that one pleased God only by living without sinning. Sin, said my mentors, caused God to remove the grace he had granted me in salvation. A perfect life was the only logical way to please God. But I found it impossible to live perfectly.

Martin Luther, as a young Catholic, once accepted this same delusion that to have favor with God one must live without sin. Luther's confessor, irritated with Martin's great zeal to be free of guilt, once told him not to come back until he had some sins worth reporting. Unlike Luther, I had no one to set my own troubled spirit to rest. Dogged by guilt and the certain knowledge that I would sin again, my life became increasingly miserable. My constant failure to live without sin fostered a neurotic need to know how God felt about me. Could I ever be sure he still loved me and that I was in his keeping? Nourished on a theology of guilt, I spent my early years as a Christian never really being confident about my relationship with God.

How foolish is all our emphasis on God's justice, if we do not balance it with God's mercy! A God who is only holy and perfect is a God whose ideals are unattainable. Such a God loses touch with those who need a God of mercy. None of us want to worship an imperfect God, but we feel secure in the presence of God only if he is willing to behold our own imperfect lives through forgiving and merciful eyes.

And make no mistake about it, God wants all who come to him to be secure. The Almighty is not flattered by neurotic and peaceless children who reflect poorly on the character of the indwelling Christ. It is not so much that God punishes his peaceless children. He is, rather, pained by them.

Forever in my mind is a church member who had a seven-year-old who needed psychiatric treatment. Her parents loved her, but they seemed to duck their head in the admission that their daughter needed such heavy psychiatric help at such a young age. Every parent wants to boast of moral children who trust them, and in their trust find the peace of mind to explore the joy of their young years.

God has set us free in Christ. As we trusted him to save us, we are to trust him to keep us in spite of our sin.

God does not ask us to live perfectly, but he does ask us to agree to his ownership and control. We make this agreement when we first turn our lives over to him. In Scripture this is referred to as a covenant. God loves us and is prepared to promise us eternal life if we will promise him our whole selves.

Today we are more used to thinking of contracts than covenants. Since human trust is unsure and security is a perishable item, we have invented the contract as our own guarantee of happiness.

We sign many contracts during our lives. Each of them is a witness to our interest, to our security. The G.M.A.C. contract is security for our auto loan. The lease agreement is security for our dwelling place. A job contract is security for our employment. Contracts are founded on the principle that security comes from predictable circumstances. Documents offer physical verification of our agreements.

Contract is a formidable and cold word for what occurs when Christ enters a life. I prefer *covenant* because it is a warmer term. Contracts define agreements made in the world of commerce and finance. Covenants define agreements made in the realm of spiritual and interpersonal relationships. As the marriage covenant ends the separation of bride and groom by supplying them with a new and intimate togetherness, so the grace covenant ends our separation from God. In fact, the purpose of the grace covenant is to end the alienation we have from God before we come to know Christ.

Breaking Down the Walls

Remember that *covenant* means an agreement between two. But before an agreement can occur, the two who make the agreement must sit together in peace, having settled all their hostility so that there will be no shadows on their relationship.

Many times our alienation from God stems from hostility! It is as though we arrogantly dare God to grant us meaning or happiness. C. S. Lewis wrote in *Surprised by Joy* that God had to engulf him, and only then did God quit being a target for his hostility.

What I wrote in *Surprised by Joy* was that "before God closed in on me, I was in fact offered what now appears a moment of wholly free choice." But I feel my decision was not so important. I was the object rather than the subject in this affair. I was decided upon. I was glad afterwards at the way it came out, but at the moment what I heard was God saying, "Put down your gun and we'll talk."[1]

While it is probably safer to be angry with God than to ignore him, all meaningful fellowship with God is impossible until we are willing to reason with him about our hope. "Come now, let us reason together, says the LORD: though your sins are like scarlet, they shall be as white as snow" (Is 1:18) is an entreaty to discuss our personal cleansing rationally. We must allow God to get off gunpoint before the dialog of faith can begin.

People through the ages have struggled with God. Augustine struggled against God. Paul at his conversion is accused by God of kicking against the goads. On the Damascus Road he at last surrendered his quarrel with the Almighty and came to know the indwelling Christ. Paul, in Ephesians 2:12-17, says that those of us who have come to Christ have been accepted (even though we are not Jewish) because God has taken steps to end our "enmity" (KJV) with him. In simple words, God knew that we were separated from him, and he did everything necessary to end our alienation. In the death of Christ, God has broken down the barrier of sin that separates us from himself.

The word *alienation* indicates a separating or a pulling apart. The alienation described in Ephesians 2:11-22 is long-standing. It grew out of the idea that Israel was the Chosen People. To call ourselves chosen is to imply that others are the Rejected People. Those who were not Jews were thought of as outcasts and called dogs.

When alienation ends, the resulting togetherness is always joy! This elation first flooded our lives the moment we accepted Christ and entered into union with him. But what really happened? There were certainly times after our initial union with Christ when we still felt alien and unhappy. We were supposed to be saved and know the resulting joy, but the joy eluded us. We discovered that although the big wall of our defiance was down, we were constantly erecting little walls with the sins we committed after conversion.

Was there a difference between the big wall and the little walls? There were lots of similarities. Both tended to shut us off from God. But the big wall was eternal; if we had not allowed God to level it, union with Christ would have been impossible forever. The little walls are only temporal, but they do keep us from really enjoying our relationship with God.

We dare not imply that our tending to build barriers between ourselves and the Forgiving God can thwart our relationship with him. We are created, as Augustine said, both to glorify God and enjoy him forever. And we can enjoy him without feeling that we must be as perfect as he is.

Just as the marriage covenant permitted a new union of two separate wills, so in salvation the God who destroys walls permitted us a new spiritual intimacy with himself even though we are morally unlike him. The marriage agreement, however, is secure only as long as both parties desire the union to continue. Our relationship with God is eternal. Human willfulness will not disrupt it, but it will wreak havoc on the joy of our togetherness.

Whenever we embrace a spirit of self, we blunt the communication we enjoyed when we first came together with God. Now we must yield our new self-will to the Father and allow him to smash the smaller walls of ego and ambition and thus to restore to us uninterrupted oneness.

Covenant: Secured in Writing

As the marriage covenant is protected by civil law, so the love between Christ and ourselves is secured by divine love (Rom 8:1-4). God has laid out for all his followers his immutable covenant; if we meet the conditions, we participate in his redemption. Romans 10:9 could easily be paraphrased as the covenant of redemption by which we are made one with Christ. "If you confess with your lips that Jesus is Lord and believe in your heart that God raised him from the dead, you will be saved." We receive God's saving grace by doing two things: confessing with our mouth the lordship of Jesus Christ and believing in his resurrection. Because of what God has done, we can enter into a splendid partnership. Happiness results from the cosignature of God and man on the same line. It is fixed.

Whenever I reflect on the great number of contracts I have made in my life, I realize they are only the paper expression of two wills. For instance, when I borrowed money for my car, the desire of the banker was to earn the interest on the loan I would repay. My own desire was to have the car sooner than I could if I had to wait for my savings to grow until I could purchase it outright.

Human feeling does not, however, validate business contracts. Feeling is always secondary to the word of the agreement. No one assumes that a loan is more valid if the borrower weeps in sincerity before the loan officer. Nor is a trial legally binding because the defendant bubbles with joy before the circuit judge. It is the word of the contract and not the mood of the signer that fixes its validity. Many Christians have been at fault for assuming that emotion is indispensable to the faith agreement. "This person did not seem sincere when he believed," we say, or, "That person did not weep."

God is immutable and so are his covenants. He is not dependent on human emotion to confirm his eternal truths. The Scriptures spawn great emotion. Joy, rapture, repentance are all evidence that the Bible stirs us deeply. However, salvation is far more than a deep stirring of soul—it is guaranteed grace.

Nothing rivals the security of contracts. They are armor against our insecurity and doubt. If, for example, there is some question that a soldier has been granted a discharge from the military service, all he needs to do is produce the paper to confirm the truth. The grace covenant, in a similar way, is a Christian's defense against doubt. Should the skeptic come and ask, "How do you know you are going to heaven?" the indicted one merely produces the contract: "He who believes in the Son has eternal life; he who does not obey the Son shall not see life, but the wrath of God rests upon him" (Jn 3:36).

"Do I believe on the Son?" If the answer is yes, then I have written evidence which supports my claim to everlasting life. John 1:12 is similar evidence to the accusing skeptic that our covenant exists in writing: "But to all who received him, who believed in his name, he gave power to become children of God." Then by strength of the covenant we may ask, "Did I receive him?" If the answer is yes, we have been given the authority of an heir, and we have the evidence of his Word to demonstrate our new status.

The value of this written security is the basis of our confidence. Doubt is the great demoralizer. Everyone who is "born again" (Jn 3:3) is given the credentials of ownership; we belong to Christ by virtue of the new birth. Just as the birth certificate is a legal document to prove our age, name and parentage for the rest of our lives, so we may think of John 3 as a "new birth certificate" where we find fixed in writing the demonstration of our new life.

While we voluntarily enter into covenant with Christ (the Eternal Word), it is God (the Senior Partner) who guarantees the agreement. Were the arrangement fixed solely on our own integrity and trust, it would be an ill-kept covenant. Like

Simon Peter, we all affirm with vigor our intentions only to find that our practice of faith is fickle and weak. Joy is ours just in knowing that God both makes the bargain and secures it in himself.

God saves us in simplicity and honesty; his Word is the majestic security of love. There is no fine print. Neither are there loopholes. There are no exigencies not covered by his Word. Everything necessary to our complete salvation and ensuing happiness is included.

I am loved and I may count on it. The word *neurosis* has been expunged by life. God is predictable and so is my eternal destiny. It is like those times when we were children and fell asleep in the car on vacation. From lane to lane of traffic through a thousand hazards we slept. Our parents passed gasoline transports with high octane potential for holocaust. From state to state we slept until their loving arms took us from the auto and deposited us, still sleeping, in a strange bed we would not discover till we awoke the next morning. We slept because of the principle of deep trust. What could go wrong in a world where our parents had staked their own lives on our security?

We can see Christ as he crosses the chasm of time and hangs on the earth side of immortality. And whatever the cross says, we hear it clear enough: A God who loves a world like this can be depended upon. "We may sleep," as Macbeth said, "in spite of thunder." When my children were young I let them sleep with me on stormy nights. They might have believed I loved them had I forced them to face the roar and light in their own rooms. But when their small forms snuggled against my own, I heard their easy breathing in the night and knew the meaning of trust.

I live in a protected world. He is with me, and I know the covenant of grace is proof enough for me to say in the marketplace that I am loved. I haven't measured it all theologically, but I understand that it is forever and I am secure.

Under New Management

Surrender is our first responsibility in the relationship. We are often unhappy because we try to renege on our initial agreement with God. Having signed on the same line with the Almighty we later try to erase our name. We then turn from our obligation to the covenant and try to control our careers or ambitions. We want Christ but only as a permissive Lord who will allow us to steer our future in a direction favorable to our own well-being as we define it. Our flights of ambition wean us from the necessity of Christ as we become more self-dependent and less Christ-dependent. Finally we are mired in self-will. Life becomes unmanageable. Crises arise. Problems do not yield to a solution. Life ultimately goes out of control.

A part of the importance of Romans 8:28 is the promise of divine sovereignty. "We know that in everything God works for good with those who love him." We who have entered the grace covenant are now under new management. Our affairs are not our own. Our Father who owns both us and our affairs is a competent manager. He has the overview of our lives, seeing both beginning and end and has given us the security of knowing he is working it out to the greatest good.

But his management is possible only through the word *Lord*. It is the supremely important word of the New Testament. It is the word of his *competent* control of our lives. We often feel a need for conversion because we have not been successful at directing our own lives. We discover that our best attempt to control our destinies is like plowing the sea. We sink in the morass of our own disorganization. We become frustrated. We struggle vainly against despair. The end of all our mismanagement is defeat, just as the ultimate end of all divine management is victory.

Much of our spiritual depression after signing the grace covenant is the result of our own desire to regain control of our affairs. Having surrendered to his authority, we reassert our own from time to time. We begin to feel that our original surrender was premature. We grasp again at all we had surrendered: clutching all our old ambitions with the claws of ego.

I confess that I started this book many times before I finally wrote it. I remember that during one such attempt I became depressed as my typewriter seemed stodgy and sterile while I tried to get the book going. During one of these periods I ran into an old friend.

"What's the matter with you?" he asked.

"Oh," I replied, "I'm writing a very frustrating book."

"What about?"

"It's a book on joy," I replied.

He burst into laughter. "*You* are writing a book on joy!"

I admitted that while my demeanor was something less than what I wanted to inspire, I was indeed trying to write this very book. Ultimately, I abandoned the project altogether till I could be free from the mixed-management syndrome. As a manager, I had to admit I was a failure. The victory I sought could be realized only by willfully and deliberately abdicating control and giving it back to the Father. I realized for the first time the beauty in the old hymn:

And every virtue we possess and every victory we win

And every thought of holiness are his alone.

This happiness is not only the result of surrender to his control but also a matter of our trust.

His lordship is of the moment, and his straightening of life begins at the moment of our confession. This momentary control is registered in the confident day-by-day peace he grants to us. If we do not have this control, the skeptics are right when they accuse us of "pie-in-the-skyism." It is not that he will someday work everything together for our good, but that he is right now doing it. Right now, when the bills are unpaid, when the job is tenuous, when our health is under sentence by disease—now he is Christ the Lord, managing life according to his agreement with us.

I am disturbed when I hear believers say "Lord" thoughtlessly. Many Christians are guilty of making Christ only a figurehead while continuing to run their lives just as they did before. It may be possible to fake the lordship of Christ now, but in the days when Paul wrote the letter to Romans, *Lord* was not a word used flippantly by the church.

Romans, in the time of Christ, characteristically said, "Caesar is Lord." It was a political and patriotic custom. Failure to recognize the supreme divinity of the Caesars was a crime punishable by death. From the time of Nero Caesar down to the time of Constantine Caesar, the statement "Jesus is Lord" was judged as not merely insane but traitorous. Many Christians were put to death in the Colosseum because they refused to modify the word *Caesar* with the dignity of the word *Lord*. When martyrdom hung on the use of the word, it was used sparingly and specifically. If Busch Stadium or the Astrodome belonged to such emperors today, there might be more current respect for the word *Lord*.

To make *Lord* mean what it meant when Paul used it would be to interpret it in light of Dietrich Bonhoeffer's translation of Luke 9:23, "Come with me and die!" The lordship of Christ means that while he increases we decrease. To have his management we must give up ours.

The Resurrection: Hope Guaranteed
Belief in the resurrection is part of the contract because it is so central to Christianity's teaching. The Incarnation of God in

Christ is bound, front and back, by miracle. At the beginning of his life is the virgin birth; at the end of his life is the resurrection. The resurrection is the dead Christ becoming the living Christ, the substance of our living faith. We cannot know deathless, eternal life without the Christ in whose triumphant life our salvation is accomplished. Therefore, one may not be a Christian without confidence in this miracle, for indeed there is no Christianity otherwise.

But the overriding importance of the miracle is the hope it extends. Only if we accept the resurrection as truth is there any such thing as final hope. Examine the lives of the apostles between that first Good Friday and the first Easter Sunday morning, and see the utter despair that had settled on them when the gloom of Christ's defeat by death had overtaken them. But the joy of the living Christ came with unquenchable optimism that first Easter morning. That same optimism is ours, and it is born fresh every morning. Paul testified, "For if we have been united in a death like his, we shall certainly be united with him in a resurrection like his" (Rom 6:5). Resurrection is the victory born of Jesus' obedience to all that his beloved Father asked. Now his victory is our hope. His life is our promise and our eternal peace.

So the very mention of Christ's resurrection speaks of our own optimism. We will one day stand on our own graves and laugh a free man's laughter. Like St. Paul we will one day cry, "O death, where is thy sting? O grave, where is thy victory?" We shall then be raised by the power of God just as he was. Now the victorious aspect of this resurrection is knowing that beyond this death we will never again stand accountable for our sins. We have the Bible's promise: "There is therefore now no condemnation for those who are in Christ Jesus" (Rom 8:1). Christ has borne the penalty and judgment for our sins and we shall never again have to face them.

Therefore, when we acknowledge our faith in the living Christ, we are free from all fear that future events, however severe, can threaten us. No matter the test, even in the face of cancer or nuclear war, like Paul we may say, "I consider that the sufferings of this present time are not worth comparing with the glory that is to be revealed to us" (Rom 8:18). It is somehow like reading the last chapter of a novel first. There are no surprises. The guarantees are certain, and knowing that everything is going to end well, we can find happiness. No wonder St. Theresa called her Carmelite sisters to joy and reminded them that Christianity needed no frowning saints.

Our joy like his covenant abides forever. God does not pull us out of the waves and demand that we behave ourselves in the lifeboat or he will throw us once again into the angry sea. The rescue we have received in Christ Jesus is not merely a one-time experience. Salvation is a process as much as it is an act. Paul said we not only had been saved, but were "being saved" (1 Cor 1:18). Much of our happiness comes from the confidence that, while we are saved, our rescue is not as complete as it will one day be when we stand before the great redeeming Christ. To be saved is to be in the lifeboat and headed for the security of the port. But the fact that salvation is also a voyage means we are not quite in the harbor yet.

The lifeboats will hold us from the terror of the seas, secure until that day of our glorious and final union with Christ. Because of this great grace covenant, we are secure in the promise, "Never will I leave you; never will I forsake you" (Heb 13:5 NIV). His covenants are as enduring as his promise: "Lo, I am with you always, to the close of the age" (Mt 28:20). We have a secure agreement wherein our all-powerful Christ has promised us eternity in his presence. "My sheep hear my voice, and I know them, and they follow me; and I give them eternal life, and they shall never perish, and no one shall snatch them out of my hand. My Father, who has given them to me, is greater than all, and no one is able to snatch them out of the Father's hand" (Jn 10:27-29). God has declared himself in our interest.

Since our destiny is made secure by his promise, let us come with joy as our fitting response to him who has made us alive in Christ Jesus.

Blow on the coal of the heart,
The candles in churches are out.
The lights have gone out in the sky.
Blow on the coal of the heart
And we'll see by and by. . . .
Archibald MacLeish

Do not get drunk with wine, for that is debauchery;
but be filled with the Spirit.
Paul of Tarsus

Thus modern man, like an adolescent in profound crisis,
appears to us to present a strange and contradictory mixture.
. . . He has repressed the very principle of his inner harmony:
the Spirit.
Paul Tournier

3
The Inner Light of the Holy Spirit

A WOMAN WHO lived alone in her Bedford-Stuyvesant home died. Though the coronor found no organic reason for her death, I think the cause was neglect. She was weary of setting a single plate at the table and fixing her coffee one cup at a time. Loneliness is a slow killer, but it is a certain assassin. The old woman had written on her calendar only one phrase, "No one came today." Her death is a plea from the basic nature of man; none of us is self-sufficient.

To be a Christian does not eliminate our social needs. Isolation is the comrade of misery; communion is essential to happiness. Occasionally we hear of someone so scarred by the social machine that he withdraws to a hermitage. From time to time we may cry out for a hideaway, an escape from the press of too many people. After we have borne the brunt of some ugly social rejection, we feel we would rather have the pain of loneliness than risk further the inhumanity of human beings. But we are not created to find happiness in seclusion.

The retreat from utter loneliness can produce bizarre relationships. The old maid and her Siamese cat, Robinson Crusoe and Friday, the Odd Couple—these all suggest one thing: if there were only one other person in all the world besides me, no matter how unlike me he was, I would prefer his communion to living life in silence. We are created to communicate and we must do it. One of the severest forms of punishment in existence is solitary confinement.

Just as we must communicate with others, we must also communicate with God. Pascal once said we were created with an inner vacuum which only God can fill. Therefore, till God enters our lives we have nothing at the center of our lives.

How hungry for substance is the world about us! Western culture has developed a way of life that hurries its millions of people through tense and frantic lifestyles. We are the treadmill society whose people are kept running but are deprived of nourishment and meaning. The healing for our hurriedness cannot be found. The churches, instead of slowing the world down, seem to contribute to this immense perpetual-motion machine.

An Explosion of the Spirit

Unfortunately, not much consideration was given to the Holy Spirit for many years. Could it be that he was too inward and silent to work well in suburban softball leagues and busy church programs. Among the Bingo cards and boutique engravings, the Holy Spirit had little place in the contemporary church except where he made his own place. Therefore, in the 1960s the vital presence of the Spirit exploded from the corners of many unsuspecting denominations and became an embarrassment to church leaders who preferred to read about Pentecost than have to deal with it here and now.

A kind of cosmic Whitsunday loomed large! We saw at last

that the Holy Spirit was a full member of the Trinity. For decades, even in a revivalist and evangelical culture, he had suffered because of the church's refusal to give him space in its liturgy and teaching. Suddenly he was fully alive in what might be called by church historians of the future "The Age of the Spirit"! Many say that this explosion was created by a blasé church that had ceased to care that their congregations were suffering from an inner emptiness. Regardless, this emphasis on the infilling of the Holy Spirit was the answer to a hungry Christendom. The Spirit came in power on our embarrassingly dead formality and routine Christianity.

A similar movement began in the Catholic Church during the leadership of Pope John XXIII. Much concern had been growing that while the official liturgy of the Mass or baptism still spoke "in nomine Patris, et Filii, et Spiritus Sancti," the weakest words of that liturgy were unquestionably the last two. Pope John, in what was dubbed *aggiornamento* (remodeling) of the Catholic ecclesiology, taught that it was time for Catholicism to put some teeth back into its doctrine of the Holy Spirit.

Meanwhile a great groundswell of *aggiornamento* in regard to the Holy Spirit began to sweep the Protestant church. Episcopalians—America's respectable bridge-playing, country-club trinitarians—were among the first to experience charismatic upheaval. Raging waves of neopentecostalism began sweeping other Protestants and Roman Catholics into a new, warm sea of unity.

It is sad that a large segment of the church is unaffected by the spiritual revolution that has baptized much of Christianity with new energy. Some churches still prefer churchmanship without any supernatural dimensions. It is hard to say why. There is a defeatism in trying to speak of Christ in churches who would welcome him in as part of creeds or sermons but shut him out as a real force for the renovation of lives and church programs. Such churches become hollow museums whose curators grow content to speak his name without the slightest danger of experiencing his presence.

Those who have seen him at work anew have begun asking, "Who is the Holy Spirit? What is his relationship to the church?"

The New Testament pictures the Holy Spirit in many ways. He is teacher, guide to the will of God, the available power of God. But there are two primary roles he possesses in the lives of Christians. First, he is called "the Seal" (the evidence that we are saved and belong to God), and second, he is called "the Comforter."

The Seal of the Spirit

He is our Seal because he is the down payment of our full salvation. "In [Christ] you also, who have heard the word of truth, the gospel of your salvation, and have believed in him, were sealed with the promised Holy Spirit, which is the guarantee of our inheritance until we acquire possession of it, to the praise of his glory" (Eph 1:13-14). Though we do not yet completely possess all the benefits that will come to us in Christ, we do have the Spirit, as promised, and he guarantees that the rest will indeed be ours as well.

The Spirit also offers sure evidence that we are adopted as children of God. And what is the only way I can know that I am a child of the King? The inner witness of the Spirit!

How hungry the world is for this! Ours is an orphaned generation, eager to be a part of a great family. Philosophy has cut away all serious belief in God, and we have entered an age of amputated men and women longing for deep relationships. The age of the Spirit has come. The desperate need to be part of a loving and caring family is now possible. The great truth of the Spirit of God is that we are not orphans: we are sons. "For you did not receive a spirit that makes you a slave again to fear, but you received the Spirit of sonship. And by him we cry, '*Abba,* Father.' The Spirit himself testifies with our spirit that we are God's children" (Rom 8:15-16 NIV). This witness leaves us holding the firm, ripe fruit of the finished work of Christ. The revelation is complete. The presence of God is universally with all believers, and we are one in his Spirit. This is precisely the meaning of the word *paraclete,* the Greek word for the Spirit, "the presence." Its literal meaning is the "one called alongside," "the accompanist," "the comrade."

When the Soviets launched the first space satellite in 1957, they dubbed it *Sputnik,* Russian for "comrade" or "fellow-traveler." It circumnavigated the globe in only a few minutes, and the world was astounded. But the interesting thing about the little ball was its loyalty. It moved around the earth even as the earth hurtled through space.

It well deserved its name, "fellow-traveler." It beeped its little signal constantly and refused to be silent. It communicated its presence to the planet. In a similar way the Holy Spirit continues to affirm his presence in our lives.

This presence authenticates our claim to be Christians. All who are made new in Christ have the Holy Spirit living inside them. Moreover, his inner presence is the evidence that we are possessed, for "any one who does not have the Spirit of Christ does not belong to him" (Rom 8:9). John said, "By this we know that he abides in us, by the Spirit which he has given us" (1 Jn 3:24). And speaking of those out of Christ, Jude 19 says, "It is these who set up divisions, worldly people, devoid of the Spirit."

The Promise of His Presence
The words *Comforter* and *Counselor* speak of the enduring pres-

ence of Jesus Christ. Christ never promised us that life would always go our way, but he did promise that whether or not things went our way, he would never leave us. "Never will I leave you; never will I forsake you" (Heb 13:5 NIV).

His presence is his promise, and his Holy Spirit is the fulfillment of his eternal presence.

A Christian without the Spirit is rather like a man I once met on the street. His jaw was slack, his eyes were vacant, his shoulders rounded. His frame proclaimed his retarded nature. He talked to himself and seemed to find it adequate. He didn't have a dangerous madness—he was merely powerless. Either our worship and ministry will talk to God, or we will ignore him and move through life in retarded conversation with ourselves.

When first we came to faith, we entered into conversation with our Father. We were set on a high-frequency humanity. Our communication, like our interest, shifted plateaus. Without the Spirit our link to God would be impossible, for he is our bridge to Christ and the Father. Blot out the Holy Spirit and not only is the Trinity a distant duality, but we and God are no longer on speaking terms. He is our sole means of communication on our journey through the long night into day. He is God's presence for the pilgrimage that must otherwise be passed in silence.

Jesus said he had to ascend to the Father in order to send us the Spirit: "It is to your advantage that I go away, for if I do not go away, the Counselor will not come to you" (Jn 16:7). Christ and the disciples had a wonderful spirit of togetherness. But in electing to become one of us, Jesus had imposed some limitations on himself. Those limitations were physical and spatial. After Bethlehem, the Son of God became limited by his body to our geography; he could be in only one place at a time. If he was with believers in Antioch, he could not be with them in Rome and Athens. So to escape the geographical confines of being in human form, Jesus had to go away. Through the Holy Spirit he came back at Pentecost, as the invisible and indwelling Christ, everywhere present, in inner communion with all believers, at once.

To the apostles, the desperation of doing without Christ after sharing three years of intimacy with him must have been unbearable. Those days between the Ascension and Pentecost must have left them hungry, for the Christ was absent. But when the day of Pentecost was fully come, communion with Christ was restored, to continue uninterrupted for all time. The Holy Spirit appeared as tongues of flame above the joyous exiles of the Ascension. Then Christ moved in. The Comforter had come. Spiritual loneliness was past. The late F. Townley Lord wrote of his mother, "She knew nothing of the discussions of the scholars about the Saviour, as a historic figure, but everything of Him as a daily presence."

We are not happy, however, merely because we are indwelt by the Spirit. Rather, it is our communion with the Holy Spirit from which happiness springs. The indwelling of the Spirit begins at our conversion and extends into eternity, but our seasons of happiness come when we are living in openness before God. Briefly put, his "indwelling" is God's eternal togetherness with us. The "infilling" is God and us in conversation. Happiness comes from the latter, from a continuing communication with him.

False-Front Christianity
There are many Christians who are genuinely born again but live in utter misery because they have only a mechanical communion with God. To illustrate their plight, let us look at marriage. Marriage implies togetherness, but it does not always connote a happy togetherness. Many couples live together for years, quarreling their way between anniversaries, held to-

gether by children or mutual insecurities. In a similar way, many Christians characteristically live in defeat. They live together with God but are not on speaking terms with him. In spite of the Holy Spirit who indwells them, their relationship with God is strictly academic.

No marriage is ever whole without the emotional harmony of two wills. The bride and groom must be able to integrate their desires and directions for the marriage to be authentic. They may elect to present a false unity to the world. They may go to bridge parties (quarreling in the car both to and from) and put on a "Can-I-get-you-anything-Lovey?-No-thank-you-Sweetie" show. Under the social veneer the authentic relationship is missing.

Christians too are guilty of faking relationships. In church services they may appear to be content in their affair with God. But in reality they have not talked to him for weeks or months. Every day finds them lost in the frustration and defeat of amputated living. Ever and anon they see congenial atheists who appear to be having a better time with life than they are. They may even envy them the happiness of their unbelief. The truth is, the atheist may actually be as happy as a Christian who has lost all communion with the Inner Christ.

So the key to our happiness is not simply togetherness with God through his Holy Spirit. It is even more than the emotional integration of our will and his will: it is the displacement of our will with God's. When we try to permit both wills to inhabit one life, phoniness is the result. When we allow our will to coexist or vie for control with the will of God, we cannot have the full presence of the Holy Spirit. He cannot fill our lives when we are filled with ourselves. As one cannot have one glass completely filled with milk and completely filled with water, he fills our lives when we set aside our own desires and goals, and become content to be servants.

Obedience to the will of God, then, is deciding that we are going to be real. We are genuine only when we are obedient. Our willingness to obey his will is the evidence that he fills our lives. When we ignore him while still claiming to be Christian, we are phony.

Obedience to the divine will is an issue of righteousness. Continuing to speak in the context of marriage, Paul sets forth the important principle, "What partnership have righteousness and iniquity? Or what fellowship has light with darkness?" (2 Cor 6:14). God is totally righteous; but considering that we are innately sinful, how can we and God ever get on speaking terms? Only when we become righteous.

We are constantly trying to produce this righteousness by ourselves. We do not do very well at it, however. Sometimes we try to paste on a pious look, an expression halfway between a migraine headache and acid indigestion. Or we add a little melody to our voice when we say, "Good morning!" Our best solo attempts at trying to be good end up only being "goody."

Isaiah warns us that all our homemade righteousness is "as filthy rags." Only the righteousness which God puts into our lives places us on speaking terms with him.

The Bible tells us we are sinners. There is only one thing that commends us to God—enough honesty to admit our condition. If we take any other approach toward our sin, we become like a cancer patient clinging in futility to aspirin. We desperately need healing, but that healing is never in ourselves. It is in the Divine Spirit as he enters our lives. His healing is effective because it comes from the inside out. Our best attempts at self-healing begin on the surface of our souls and never reach the deepest levels where his healing has its beginning.

The scribes and Pharisees made God's approval their one goal; they worked hard at it. But Jesus said, "Unless your righteousness exceeds that of the scribes and Pharisees, you will never enter the kingdom of heaven" (Mt 5:20). So our finest attempt at spiritual behavior is inadequate. Our righteousness must be found in Christ and claimed in faith. Now God freely gives us his divine approval by which our own sinfulness is taken away as we come before him in complete openness.

Confession: Reopening Communication

Still, the season of complete fellowship is always under the threat of the life we lived before we were his. This old life is always our monstrous alter ego, ready in a moment to reassert its rule in our lives and relegate the Holy Spirit to second place. The struggle of the new man in Christ (Rom 7) can be fierce indeed (2 Cor 12:7-10). It is rather similar to the Bulldog Ant that the philosopher Arthur Schopenhauer describes. Schopenhauer says that should this ant be cut in half, the front and rear segments enter into a fight that is brutally savage. The head will seize the tail with its teeth, while the tail will sting the head with fury. The fight may endure for hours. At such moments the ant much resembles the Christian's inner quarrel; often with brutal and masochistic ripping he attempts to establish the control of the Holy Spirit.

But it would somehow be unfair of God to offer us no hope or escape from that lurking life we once lived before we knew Christ. Life in Christ must surely be more than the unpredictable alternation of victory and defeat. Jesus surely meant the promise, "Peace I leave with you; my peace I give to you" (Jn 14:27). And this peace is not left to our best attempt to achieve it. Rather it comes to us by the complete management of the Holy Spirit. He promises not to leave us in turmoil and frustration, a victim of our lifelong struggle with that other self we were before he came. We are whole through the Holy Spirit, who is the Great Integrator for Christians, helping us to live by one will, that we may become altogether like Jesus, in constant communion with him whom we adore.

Of course he knows our every transgression. But our openness before God means that we acknowledge our sins to him so communion can be re-established. I often find my children disobedient. Once or twice, they have tried to hide their disobedience. I knew they had behaved badly, but they were unwilling to tell me they had. I saw them suffer because they knew they had been less than I wanted them to be. I longed for them to be open with me about their misbehavior. If they failed to do this, their guilt would often keep them from talking to me at all. Even though I knew they had done something wrong, their failure to tell me about it would interrupt our usual togetherness.

The Spirit is our bridge. Without him our straining to reach God embraces only emptiness. But the bridge must be maintained. When I see crews painting the cables and girders of the Golden Gate Bridge, I understand this principle. If the piers should rust and the salt air be left to nibble at the exposed steel, it would not be long till traffic ceased. To "quench the Spirit" is to restrict our communion with God. If our goal as Christians is to live in constant communion with the Father, then it is obvious that being open before God implies consistent confession of our sins.

When we were first redeemed, our sins were all cleansed, and for the first rapturous time we knew the meaning of togetherness with God. But shortly after that time most of us experienced a strange kind of anxiety and the feeling that while we were certain about his redemption, he was in some sense remote. Then after a season of prayer and confession, the rapport was restored. We discovered that after this first, great renewal, there had to be little seasons of renewal.

One sin will not erase the relationship any more than one

argument will dissolve a marriage. But one sin will put a cloud over our togetherness and stain our communion with our Father until openness is re-established. To be cleansed we must confess our sins (1 Jn 1:9). We are made righteous altogether by the approval granted to us by God because of our openness before him.

This openness is implied in the word *confess*. The word in Greek means to "agree with." When we confess we do not ask primarily for forgiveness. Once we are saved, our sins are forever forgiven. But once we "agree with" God that we have committed such and such a sin, our honesty before him re-establishes the communication that was broken.

Our authenticity, however, cannot be based on our feelings. It must rather be based on the integrity of our confession and on our God whom we trust has forgiven us.

When Guilt Remains

Yet often guilt, the enemy of renewal, remains. It is our attempt at homemade atonement. By holding on to guilt feelings we are erroneously trying to help God do what God has already fully done in the death of Christ. Christians who are guilty of this will often say plaintively, "I asked God to forgive such and such, but I just can't *feel* that he has forgiven me." We are saying, "I doubt that God can forgive me if I merely ask." Our continued guilt feelings imply that God's grace has to be accompanied by major grieving and earnest deportment of our own to indicate our sincerity. At such times we say the cross is inadequate. Jesus could not possibly have "paid it all," so we must pay the remainder by feeling bad about ourselves.

When we cling to guilt on the basis of our feeling unforgiven, we commit a gross sin against the integrity of God. We impose our emotion and intuition against the validity of God's revelation in Scripture. God said if we would confess, then he would forgive. The matter is settled. Failing to forgive ourselves what he has already forgiven us is spiritual exhibitionism.

Frequently some sincere Christian will say to me, "I committed such and such a sin, but I asked God several times to forgive me, and now I know he has." In every case I ask him why he asks God several times to forgive what God had already forgiven at the first petition. Then I ask him to confess to God the sin of holding on to guilt when he didn't believe 1 John 1:9: "If we confess our sins, he is faithful and just, and will forgive our sins and cleanse us from all unrighteousness."

We want the feeling of being forgiven to come before we are comfortable acting forgiven. But *feeling* ought to follow *action*. E. Stanley Jones once observed that it is easier to "act yourself into a new way of thinking" than to "think yourself into a new way of acting." William James said, "Action and feeling go together, and by regulating the action . . . we can directly regulate the feeling." Therefore, when we confess our sin, let us immediately begin acting forgiven. As a result we will begin feeling openness with God.

This openness is the result of our infilling by the Holy Spirit. This is more than just his "residency in us." It is really his "presidency in us." It is expressed in the singleness of our will. When we want what he wants; he is there, fully in the center of our lives. When he is in complete control, the interior struggle of Romans 7 is gone. When he presides, our former life and nature lie dormant, and our new life in Christ exists in the same wonder and love we knew when first we met our Lord and Savior.

While he is in control of our lives, we are as much like the Son of God as it is humanly possible to be. As he lived, we live: in harmony with the Father, we stand free from guilt and sin. We know utter happiness, for we are completely open to God

At these moments, we truly fulfill God's intentions for our lives, and we walk in joy.

In the last chapter I wrote about covenant grace. I pointed out that both our salvation and our fellowship with God rest on the finished work of our Savior. Our continuing honesty about our sin is needed to make our peace and joy secure.

Without confession there is nothing genuine in Christian happiness. To be authentic is to be totally dependent on life by a single will. Let us completely confess our sins and move in unbroken communication with him. Liberated by this constant renewal, we shall make obvious our oneness with God. Happiness will be the witness of our lives in wholeness.

> But how shall I speak of the glories I have since discovered
> in the Bible? For years I have read it with an ever-broadening
> sense of joy and inspiration; and I love it as I love no other book.
> **Helen Keller**

> What you want is a philosophy that will not only exercise
> your powers of intellectual abstractions, but will make
> some positive connection with this actual world.
> **William James,** Pragmatism

> It always rains on our generation.
> **Lucy to Linus**

4
The Mastery of Circumstance

HOW OFTEN, WHEN someone asks us how we are doing, do we reply, "All right, under the circumstances"? But have we ever thought about what we are saying? For God never intended that we live under circumstances, to be crushed by them. Godly living aims at triumph. Still, all too often we lose the struggle with the circumstances of life. We become tangled in the webs of problems that steal the stamina and enthusiasm we want to mark our walk of faith.

Startlingly, God, in changing our lives through faith, often leaves the circumstances which surround us exactly as they were. The number and the intensity of our problems after salvation are at least equal to and perhaps greater than before our conversion. The difference is that we no longer have to stand alone.

God's Word of Care
The Bible is the instrument God has given us for dealing with

our circumstances. It is far more than the devotional pastime of Christians. The mere existence of the Bible declares that God does care about us. The coming of Christ in human form says that while God is a spirit (Jn 4:24) and is wholly above our predicament (Is 55:8-9), he is deeply concerned about us. In his Son, God has opted for identity with his world. He cares when we are crushed by the furious onrush of life in which we, his children, are often trapped and hurt.

Transcendence means God is set apart from us. But in Christ God became a man and ended his lofty, lonely vigil. Since Calvary, no one can say God has a comfortable or detached transcendence. Not just the Passion narratives but all the Bible says that God loves this world. When the slaves cried out in the land of Goshen, God sent his servant Moses to say, "Let my people go" (Ex 5:1). Nor did God care for the Jews only. He was burdened for everyone: Amos reminds us there were other slaves whom God loved. "Did I not bring up Israel from the land of Egypt, and the Philistines from Caphtor and the Syrians from Kir?" (Amos 9:7).

Jesus came calling God "Father," and we are heirs of the dynamic idea of the eternal Almighty as our own Parent. St. Paul said in Romans 8:15 that in Christ we "did not receive the spirit of slavery to fall back into fear, but . . . the spirit of sonship. . . . We cry, 'Abba! Father!' " No parent can bear to see his or her children in pain—even when their suffering is of their own making. God aches as any parent would when his children are hurt. In Christ, God delivers us as he has delivered the oppressed of all ages from the difficulty of their circumstances. The Hebrew-Christian God is a God who saves from meaninglessness those who adore him.

Problems which ensnare our lives are real problems; because they are so complex, they know no easy solution. Our circumstances never lie neat and orderly, stacked and catalogued for easy handling. Our problems are always tangled and inter-twined—clotted like cold spaghetti. Like the fabled tar baby of Uncle Remus, the more we struggle to kick free, the worse we are ensnared in our sticky difficulties.

Further, no two believers handle problems alike. Some seem to smile positively and walk out under their own power. The fiery circumstances that call forth the best in some people destroy others. Yet the issue of victory or defeat does not lie in *our* power or weakness. The overcoming answer ultimately lies in the use of *his* power. Both the victorious and the defeated have access to this same overcoming power.

We should not be tempted to trust the ordinary channels of popular promoters and positivists. Much is written and spoken on the various schemes that lead to personal power, and all of them focus on managing circumstances. Yet those in the Bible who found victory did not find it in their own resources. Indeed they seemed to triumph in spite of their weaknesses. Consider a few of those who trusted God. David, small and inept for battle, challenges Goliath and wins! Blind Samson grinds for the Philistines, but wins! Moses, the tongue-tied shepherd, stands up to the Pharaoh and wins! Jesus, who on the cross looked like history's greatest loser, stands up to Satan and wins!

The Bible is the story of the weak who learned that God triumphs in the midst of our weakness. The entire saga of Scripture is a study in the victory of those who follow God and depend on him.

The Christian army, however, loses a lot of battles because the soldiers are afraid. We are intimidated by life. We spend far too much time complaining and too little time simply trusting God and going on with the battle. The natural consequence of these fears is disobedience! I used to think that the intrigue and the enjoyment of sin made folks disobey God. But I don't think so anymore. I think that we disobey God because we are afraid to attempt to obey.

Fear draws our gaze from Christ's competence to our own inadequacy. Like Simon on the waves, we find our untried confidence quickly dissipating, leaving us at the mercy of the storm, cut off from the Christ whose image empowers us to walk on our circumstances and whose absence sinks us in defeat.

Strong in Weakness

Our victory over defeat is the splendor of believing: having faith, we involve God in our circumstances. We call on God for strength to face our problems and deliver us from our milieu instead of trying to work our own way through our affairs, leaving God a mere speculation. In everyday life we demonstrate by faith that in practical issues God becomes incarnate in our lives once more.

Academics discuss and define God. They lecture on his nature or debate his holiness. But the aloof God of the philosophers is not the God of Abraham, Isaac and Jacob. The former is a God of sterile study; the latter is the personal Lord of all human circumstance.

Too many of us believers are unhappy because we know only the academic God, the God of the confirmation class. We know he is triune, holy and just. But we have not discovered his involvement in our lives. God is shackled to musty abstractions. He is inconsequential in a world where eggs are overpriced and closing quotations are eroding corporate enterprise.

In the Bible God makes no attempt to appear nonpartisan. He is "pro-me." With all his power, he chooses to stand in *my* defense (Rom 8:31). I am his. He loves his own to the full extent of his power. Here in my needs he demonstrates the solidarity of the covenant we made at salvation.

The pro-me God becomes the overcomer God as we discover all we can about ourselves. Learning our strengths, and particularly our weaknesses, teaches us to abandon our self-reliance for his overcoming power. Knowing where our limits lie usually comes through earnest effort and disappointment, trial and failure—often bitter failure. Facing personal lack of power is painful, but every failure contains the seeds of knowledge of good and evil. This fuller knowledge of ourselves often turns into bitterness toward those who disappoint us or even toward God himself. We may be prone to indict him as though he were responsible for our failure. How wise we would be to see that often the culprit in all our suffering is ourselves. How true the cliché: "We have met the enemy and he is us!" Byron recognized this principle when he wrote:

The thorns that I have reaped
Are of the tree I planted,
They have torn me and I bleed:
I should have known what fruit
Would spring from such a seed!

God is a kind creator who wants to draw us to himself to complete within us what we find missing. He is not our adversary but our advocate. God is a creator of such power that no Christian need be weak, for power is plenteous within himself to enable us to live at the heights.

Once we learn the limits of our own power, we learn a corollary—God's power knows no limits. That's why Paul could write, "I can do all things in him who strengthens me" (Phil 4:13). You see, Paul had defined the limits of his power in Romans 7:18: "For I know that nothing good dwells within me, that is, in my flesh." Paul gloried in the power in his life. His own limitations had been supplanted by the unlimited God. And understanding that his weaknesses were opportunities for the demonstration of God's greatness, he actually thanked God for his weaknesses: "He said to me, 'My grace is sufficient for you, for my power is made perfect in weakness.' I will all the more gladly boast of my weaknesses, that the power of Christ may rest upon me. For the sake of Christ, then, I am content with weaknesses, insults, hardships, persecutions, and calamities; for when I am weak, then I am strong" (2 Cor 12:9-10). Once we understand how weak we really are, we are set to apprehend the superior, overcoming power of God.

God's pro-me principle becomes our basic assumption. God is for us, and he is working all of our circumstances toward his own ultimate goals for our lives. These circumstances may cause us pain, but they are all part of God's pro-me plan by which he molds our destiny.

The Right to Use God's Power

The children of Israel, after their hasty departure from Egypt, found themselves trapped between the chariots of Rameses and the inky waters of the Red Sea. There seemed to be no deliverance from the circumstances. Then Moses waved his rod over the sea, and it was divided by the Lord (Ex 14:21). God led the fugitives right down through the midst of their circumstances, and they were delivered. Even the Egyptians acknowledged that God was definitely partisan, for they said, "Jehovah is fighting for them and against us" (Ex 14:25 LB).

In the New Testament there is a time when the disciples are frightened by a storm. When they wake Jesus, he rebukes them because their faith has failed the test of circumstance. He calms the waves (Mt 8:26). His indignation with the disciples arises from their attempt to meet their problems with adrenalin only. God, in this night of fear, declares he is for the apostles. They were not to cower before life's storms. When the situation grew ugly, they were not to retreat into their frantic nervous systems, but appeal to the authority of Christ.

Since God created us and all the material universe, there is no situation over which his authority is not sovereign. On one occasion when Francis Schaeffer was flying across the ocean, two motors on one wing failed. Gradually the plane settled toward the ocean. When the airplane was skimming the waves and about to crash, Schaeffer, who had been praying for God to start the motors, felt the comforting jar of the sleeping engines as they flamed to life.[1] Miraculously the aircraft regained its lost altitude. Can airplane engines be started by prayer? Emphatically, yes! There are no circumstances over which God is not sovereign.

Jesus taught that if we have faith as a grain of mustard seed, there are no grand threats to our security. If Mount Everest itself bars our way, that mountain is movable (Mt 17:30). When Jesus said, "Behold, I have given you authority to tread upon serpents and scorpions, and over all the power of the enemy; and nothing shall hurt you" (Lk 10:19), he meant it. His authority is ours.

The word for *power* here is the Greek word *exousia*. Though sometimes interpreted "power," it literally means "authority" or "right." When we are converted, we are given the right to use God's power in Christ's name against every threat. Yet in my experience I know few Christians who boldly use the authority that is theirs. I like the excitement of the returning seventy in Luke 10, for they were reporting with enthusiasm that even devils were subject to them. They had placed their confidence in God and trusted him to pave their destinies with grace. What a contrast we present! Most of us are not conquerors but victims of our difficulties.

To encounter life's obstacles, discipline is mandatory. Our power will be largely determined by our knowledge and use of the Bible and the power it claims over practical difficulties. I envision our minds as a checkerboard of storage bins that represent the memory bank of our minds. I call this memory bank the "Frame of Reference" which is nothing more than stored Bible knowledge. In each of these "pigeonholes" of thought we store up the scriptural munitions for fighting specific problems.

When we first knew Christ, the memory banks of our minds were virtually empty. As we began to study and grow, we began to fill them with knowledge. The more mature we became, the fuller grew our mental filing area with the substance of our newly learned Scripture. The more we studied, the more extensive our frame of reference became. With each stage of growth, we increased our possession of the astounding authority of the Bible.

Scripture and Temptation

Let's make it practical: Perhaps when we look lingeringly at the opposite sex, we become tempted toward mental indulgence. We are not defenseless, however, if we have made Bible study a part of our lifestyle. From our mental filing cabinet we withdraw this truth: "You have heard that it was said, 'You shall not commit adultery.' But I say to you that every one who looks at a woman lustfully has already committed adultery with her in his heart" (Mt 5:27-28). Here our sense of moral obligation is corrected by God's Word, and we direct our lives to more wholesome considerations. Most threatening circumstances withdraw when confronted by scriptural authority, especially if we, as disciplined students, determine that we will obey all of God's commands.

If, when we are working on our income tax, we are tempted to "shade" our 1040 form dishonestly, if we are in danger of yielding to the lure of a fat refund check, we draw out of one of those Bible storage banks "You shall not bear false witness" (Ex 20:16). With this bit of information, we should then make our assertion against evil. This Scripture becomes our best defense. Once again ours is the victory that comes from the authority of the Book.

To build such a frame of reference requires study. As we learned in chapter one, study is the job of the disciple. The result? Happiness through the mastery of life. No wonder Paul said, "Study to show thyself approved" (2 Tim 2:15 KJV), and Peter said, "Always be prepared to make a defense to any one who calls you to account for the hope that is in you" (1 Pet 3:25).

One of the clearest examples of the use of this frame of reference is the temptation of Jesus. In every temptation Jesus answered Satan with a portion of Deuteronomy. Let's examine his circumstances. First, the devil tempts him to make stones into bread after Jesus has gone six weeks without food. Jesus, however, chooses to trust God and his provision for his needs rather than take matters into his own hands. He chooses to remain weak to show the power of God. He meets this circumstance by drawing Deuteronomy 8:3 out of his frame of reference: "Man does not live by bread alone, but . . . by everything that proceeds out of the mouth of the LORD."

Tempted next to undertake a short cut to Messiahship by leaping safely from the Temple pinnacle, Jesus drew from his frame of reference Deuteronomy 6:16: "You shall not put the LORD your God to the test." Third, when he was tempted to worship Satan in order to become the emperor of all empires at the right hand of Satan, he drew Deuteronomy 10:20 from the frame of reference and said, "You shall fear the LORD your God; you shall serve him and cleave to him." Following his mastery of these fierce challenges, the Scriptures say that "angels came and ministered unto him."

The New Testament makes clear that no areas are off limits to God's authority. There are no circumstances not subject to his control; whatever we must face, he has faced before, and he will not allow us to undergo any temptation for which he does not fortify our lives. Along with the personal strength he supplies, we also gain victories over life's entanglements by learning to meet these challenges with the fruit of our own Bible discipline. The wonderful thing is that so many of the temptations that confront us in life are mentioned in the Bible and answered specifically. By adding these texts to our frame of reference we add to our arsenal of defense. Psalm 119:11 says our frame of reference is our authority over all such eventualities: "I have laid up thy word in my heart, that I might not sin against thee."

A good memory bank of Scripture will operate for us in two directions. It will provide a good defense against the secular encroachments of the immediate context of our living. It will also give us additional weaponry so we can advance on our world with a militant hope. Let us examine the offense and the defense the memory bank provides.

The Defense of Our Faith

As young Christians we experience a joyous if fledgling enthusiasm for sharing with others the glory of the Christ life. But often our eagerness runs up against skepticism, and before long our zeal is dissipated. I remember a parable about a man who wanted to teach the sparrows in his garden to sing instead of chatter. So he bought a canary and hung its cage in his backyard. The canary sang enthusiastically for a while against the chatter of the sparrows. But somehow the bird became discouraged and his determination failed. Soon the sparrows had taught the canary their raucous speech. He had lost his song.

This is unfortunately the picture of many new Christians. Their determination to teach the world their new joy gets lost in the secular din, and many lose their song. With their lost song goes their identity as disciples. The world cannot take

Christ out of our lives, but it can secularize us so that we soak up the social dyes, and our exterior coloring becomes about the same as that of the person who has never known Christ.

Our resistance to the secular is a matter of diet. Physiologically speaking, a person's immunity to disease is dependent to a large degree on nutrition. Those of us who eat improperly are physically unprepared to deal with a good healthy virus or a stout malaria microbe. Spiritually we can also suffer from infrequent intake or from improper balance. Mentally, too, we are addicted to junk food that does not fortify our minds for struggle. We become a target for spiritual illness. We lose our immunity to defeat.

Jeremiah realized that spiritual health was dependent on a proper diet, for he wrote: "Thy words were found, and I ate them, and thy words became to me a joy and the delight of my heart; for I am called by thy name, O Lord, God of hosts" (Jer 15:16). Elsewhere Jeremiah describes the weakness of the people of God when they refuse to feed on his Word (Jer 25:1-11). Jeremiah does not say why they rejected the Word, but the ensuing verses teach that without the proper spiritual diet, they have no resistance to the world and they suffer terrible identity crises.

We suffer such a crisis whenever we claim to be the people of God but bear no spiritual resemblance or moral likeness to the Father. The next step of our atrophy is the abandonment of realism. Our very testimonies become dishonest and we cry out, "Peace, peace," when we have no peace. When we become thoroughly secularized, we may still use words like *peace* and *joy* which once described our experience with God. But these words have been displaced by our new acceptability in the alien world. Our words become an attempt to convince ourselves and others. Those who have peace don't always talk of peace. But often those in utter turmoil do.

Immunization feeds on a negative principle. A little case of measles or diphtheria is given directly into the bloodstream. The healthy person's natural defenses deal with the alien intrusion and protect him or her against a stronger attack in the future. One blister spares the person from a raging case of smallpox. In this same way many believers get only a little case of salvation that keeps them from getting the fullness of grace and joy all their lives.

Faithful study habits fortify us and keep up our resistance to the secular world. I am not suggesting we withdraw from the world or from meaningful social involvement. We must live as salt and light in society if there is ever to be a hope of saving the world. But there is no hope at all for the world's redemption if we cannot live as ambassadors whose final allegiance is one world away. Study will strengthen our ability to counter the influence of secular decay on our commitment.

Feeding on the Word, Not Each Other

Twice Scripture condemns Christians for refusing to develop mature appetites. Paul was disenchanted with those who were biblically undernourished. He castigated the Corinthians for desiring an infantile diet of milk and refusing the meat of the Word (1 Cor 3:1-3). The writer of the letter to the Hebrews also expressed disappointment in those who never grew enough to be teachers within the church (Heb 5:11-14). They were always learning the elementary truth of the gospel. They never matured enough to taste the excellence of the deeper, hidden truths of Christ.

Paul said some people of his day were ever learning but never able to know the truth (2 Tim 3:6-7). Modern Christianity is likewise condemned. There is little serious Bible study. Therefore, Christianity is infantile. The advice of 2 Peter 3:18 is largely ignored: "Grow in the grace and knowledge of our

Lord and Savior Jesus Christ."

The *fellowship* of our churches is evident testimony to our immaturity. Quarreling and wrangling are done chiefly by those who have not yet grown up. We are somewhat like the Children's Crusade who dared with juvenile enthusiasm to think they could take the Holy Land back from the Turks. The whole effort ran afoul for want of maturity.

Remember Melanchthon's illustration of the wolves who were about to enter into war with the dogs? An old scout was sent to check on the advance of the dogs. He came back to report that the wolves had nothing to fear. The dogs as they advanced were nipping and snarling and biting at each other. They could never seriously threaten the wolves, even though the dogs were greater in number.

This is a sad picture of the immaturity of today's Christian army. Undernourished by the Word, we have not matured. In our enthusiasm to win the world, our immaturity has set brother against brother so often that our energy is dissipated. Consider that sad congregation at Corinth. In the heart of a great city, so hungry for Christian meaning, the disciples were undisciplined in the Bible and quarreled savagely. Their very division left them unable to attract others who were spiritually in need.

Paul reminded another church racked by spiritual malnutrition that congregational cannibalism would leave the church a victim of its own appetite for argument and strife. "But if you bite and devour one another take heed that you are not consumed by one another" (Gal 5:15). When Christians quit feeding on the Word, they often begin feeding on each other.

When an army is hungry, there is talk of mutiny among the soldiers. Around our house my wife and I are most edgy when we are both on a diet. Under normal circumstances we relate quite well. But when we go with less food than we are used to for a few days, the most incidental of irritations can become inflammable.

I realize how true this is for the body of Christ when I think of the minor issues that have set congregations afire with hate and inner struggle. Churches have split over where to set the flowers or who will play the piano or whether or not to have a Good Friday service. Those who give their energies to such shallow issues have not given themselves to study. Thus when little problems confront them, they are readily defeated because they don't have the knowledge of the Bible necessary to deal in Christlike ways with the issues.

The Sword of Action

But the mastery of circumstance is not just a matter of our defense. It is an issue of our advance also. We are not to be content with our struggle against worldly corruption, even if we are successful. "Go therefore" (Mt 28:19) is Christ's order. Take hold of circumstances and change them!

In describing the armaments of Christian soldiers in Ephesians 6, Paul names equipment designed to protect us from our worldly milieu and against our adversary, the devil. But the passage ends by reminding us to take "the sword of the Spirit, which is the word of God" and advance (Eph 6:17).

The wise soldier would train with a sword and then use it. Imagine a soldier who kept his sword on the buffet, dusted it and polished it occasionally but never practiced with it. He would be defenseless in any conflict. Such is the case of the bibliolater. He reveres the Bible as a kind of relic cabinet containing a lock of baby's hair, a faded pressed carnation from grandpa's casket, or the children's birth certificates.

The Bible is not an amulet but a sword. The word Paul uses in Ephesians 6:17 for "sword" is *machaira*. The *machaira* was a short, two-edged blade made famous by the Roman infantry.

Many of the conquered people laughed when they first saw the *machaira* of the Roman legionnaires. Their swords seemed so short in comparison with the great long swords of their contemporaries. There was, for instance, the *romphaia* of the Thracians (Lk 2:35)—a long, impressive weapon that proved unwieldy in any close combat by reason of its size. But the short *machaira* was deadly because of its maneuverability. Combat never seemed to become too congested for the short weapon to be effective.

In Hebrews 4:12 this same word is found again: "For the word of God is living and active, sharper than any two-edged sword." We have been given the most effective of all weapons —the *machaira* of God. If we learn its wisdom and chart its truth, we will advance. No situation will be desperate because God's Word will cut a path through the difficulties and problems before us.

If we give ourselves to the study of the Word of God, we will be given the mastery of circumstance. Remember the epitaph from Hosea 4:6: "My people are destroyed for lack of knowledge; because you have rejected knowledge, I reject you." So study your way to the mastery of life. Know his Word that you may stand. In the consistency of your victories will come the consistency of your happiness.

If mankind is to escape its programmed self-extinction,
the God who saves us will not descend from the machine:
he will rise up again in the human soul.
Lewis Mumford

They . . . found the man from whom the demons had gone,
sitting at the feet of Jesus, clothed and in his right mind.
Luke the Physician

But dinosaurs were handicapped by insufficient brains.
Paul Ramsey, Reflections on Dostoevski

5
The Dynamic Mind

OUR MINDS HIDE. Only occasionally do we open them to the scrutiny of anyone else. Our thinking is not always true to the mood pictured on our faces. Our thoughts often play the hypocrite to our speech and actions. Our minds deceive those who do not doubt our sincerity. Often we smile at our antagonists while our minds, in unseen anger, are spitting and hissing. Here in the fissures of our gray matter we make all the final decisions as to whether we will disclose our true selves or continue hiding from those who only thought they knew us. But our minds cannot be false to our faces for long without risking a splintering of our egos and paying the price of mental illness.

The mind which is unified in purpose, however, offers the world an honest face whose image reflects integrity. The mind made whole by Christ becomes an exciting force within the disciple who exercises it with study and prayer. Dynamic

Christians live with growing minds. This is the gift of the Spirit of God who wills for us a singleness of purpose, disciplined commitment to learning and understanding God's will for his world. Too often, however, Christians also find themselves facing emotional problems and the threat of mental illness. How is this possible? Where have we gone wrong?

Who's Responsible?

The modern mind has achieved great things, but its accomplishments have been counterbalanced by a general ethos of misgiving. There is an epidemic of schizophrenia. This rash of mental illness is as ordinary to our enlightened times as the plague was in yesterday's Europe.

Dealing with the head is now the number one medical concern in our country. Neurotics, psychotics and deviates all have a need for professional help. One reason why people commit themselves to psychiatric care is that they feel there is a proper set of dynamics by which the mind should operate. They sense a need for those dynamics and turn in desperation to clinical psychiatry.

The psychiatrist is not a witch doctor who can supply instant mental health by psychological magic. There are, however, broad principles for healing disoriented minds.

One is that we need to accept responsibility for our mental state. A dynamic mind does not sidestep accountability. In many ways modern psychology is a science in flux. Previously the primary treatment was the "transference" method. The patients went in, told the doctor how they felt about the past and then projected their problems in transference onto their analyst.

Thomas Harris, author of *I'm OK, You're OK*, says that the Freudian method of transference is irresponsible and does little good. William Glasser, another popular voice on the contemporary scene, has gone a step further and suggested that there is a more basic fault. There is no mental illness, at least in the traditional understanding of the word. Certain mental disorders are physical in nature and can be treated with drugs or therapy, but there is no such thing as a mental illness that can be treated merely by psychotherapy. In Glasser's system patients are made responsible for their future by helping them see that they are responsible for their present and certainly their past. Patients must face reality. Doctors cannot cure because patients are not sick. They have merely accepted an unreal view of themselves and the world.

Glasser tells how on one occasion a woman came to his office and said, "I'm here, Doctor. Do psychiatry." Such a viewpoint makes the doctor accountable for the patient's hang-ups and cure.

St. Paul seemed to counsel young Timothy with this "Glasseresque" logic. He reminded him that God has not given to us a "spirit of fear; but of power, and of love, and of a sound mind" (2 Tim 1:7 KJV). Each of us is responsible for only one mind, and its health is up to us.

Wayne Dyer has encouraged each of us to "pull our own strings." His thesis is that we are responsible for our own success and failure. When life presses us into weird psychological shapes, it is foolish to pronounce judgment on life. Our psychological shape is our responsibility. We are the guardians of our minds, and to a large degree we regulate the health of our thinking.

What about Christians? Do we have problems dealing with the mind? Are we immune to mental disintegration and conflict? Do we have peptic ulcers? Do we consult psychiatrists? Gulp tranquilizers? Spend time in mental wards? Of course! But God can break through these problems as he can any others.

The Mind of Christ

Since our mind alone is incapable of discovering Christ's dynamic, the only alternative is to opt for mind renewal: "Do not be conformed to this world but be transformed by the renewal of your mind that you may prove what is the will of God, what is good and acceptable and perfect" (Rom 12:2). It is possible for us to have only one of two minds operating at a time. We may have the mind of Christ, or we may operate by corrupted minds (see also Eph 4:17 and Tit 1:15). But mark the hidden dangers in the choosing: "The mind that is set on the flesh is hostile to God; it does not submit to God's law" (Rom 8:7). That is, the unregenerate mind is self-managing.

Mental management, sometimes called influence, consists of two types: instant influence and lingering, subliminal influence. Instant influence affects us when we are given orders by our boss or our mate or the police officer in the center of the intersection. Our brain receives the order, evaluates it, processes it and alerts the muscles necessary for carrying out the order. While our reaction may seem more like a reflex than a mental process, our minds are being managed.

But our minds are also affected by more subliminal influences. Why, for instance, did I choose 7-Up at the vending machine? Did I make the decision in freedom? Why did I reject Coke, Dr. Pepper and orange soda? Possibly I was acting out of the unregistered direction of seventy-five TV commercials and twenty-five billboards that I did not notice at the time. Thus I was manipulated mentally and did not even realize it.

Because our minds determine our whole lives, our mental choices are of supreme importance. When we submit to the mind of Christ, we are under the best mental management.

Wanting What He Wants

The mind of Christ, like every other mind, includes two things:

knowledge and will. Since we have already discussed the importance of knowledge in the mastery of circumstance, let us proceed to an understanding of will. Our will reflects what we desire. Therefore, we cannot have the mind of Christ until we want what he wants.

Jesus was also our example of how, if we are to find ultimate meaning, knowledge and will must be submitted to him whose goals lead finally to glory. Jesus' will for himself was completely aligned with what the Father wanted. Likewise, we also must align our will with that of Jesus.

The inherent danger in attaining the mind of Christ is presumption. Many of us presume that what we want to do and what Christ wants us to do are the same thing. Our clever consciences may even be able to convince us that our carnal desires are little different from what Christ wants.

The mind of Christ, therefore, must be used with integrity. Paul taught that with renewed minds we should always struggle "to stand mature and fully assured in all the will of God" (Col 4:12). We are to strive to keep this world from squeezing our minds into its way of thinking. For we have been invaded by a new will that is continually renewed. Nothing short of this is an acceptable standard of commitment.

But how is it possible for us to know all that God wants? Much of God's will is clearly marked in Scripture. This does not require any anguish of soul to discover. It is God's will for everyone to be saved (2 Pet 3:9), to be sanctified (1 Thess 4:3), to give thanks for everything—even adversity (1 Thess 5:18) and to do good works (1 Pet 2:15).

But not everything that is his will is so clearly marked. At many junctures we must search for it on broader, unspecified principles. In some few cases we have to agonize with the Spirit for direction. But we can be confident that God will answer our prayer which is "thy will be done." He will do this because we have the mind of Christ—the implanted will of the Son of God.

"Kosher" Sins

There is, however, a major threat to the lordship of Christ in our minds—attitude sins. To explain what I mean, let me distinguish attitude sins from "kosher" sins. Kosher in Hebrew thought has to do with cleanliness. The Pharisees concentrated on outward cleanliness and missed its inward significance. In the same way, Christians emphasize external righteousness to the exclusion of a more substantive inwardness. Jewish laws included taboos against breaking the Sabbath, eating pork and going to Gentile parties. These are sins so outward they are clearly visible. "Kosher" Christian behavior frequently prohibits such things as bridge, snuff, port and the tango. These are the overt sins most frequently found on Christian no-no lists. Protestant evangelists major on these because they are outward and easy to identify.

To be occupied with negative values in preaching against kosher sins often builds negative people, just as mining coal makes for blackened miners. Remember how difficult it was to learn how to ride a bicycle? When we tried to miss the rocks in our path by concentrating on them, inevitably we hit them. To ride and enjoy riding, we must become free from focusing on the rocks and seek the path instead.

We become good by pursuing the good and not by avoiding evil. The pursuit of God is the positive hunger for the will of Christ. The will of Christ is his completed kingdom among men. This is why Jesus said that once we had made the kingdom our priority, we were living positively and everything else would "be added unto us."

One of Jesus' objections to the kosher laws of his day was that many of the taboos grew out of human hang-ups rather than the attitudes of God. A German evangelical and an American evangelical of my acquaintance had met and were discussing what a Christian should or should not do. The American was distressed that the German drank; the German that the American smoked. The German said, "Sometimes when I think about the nondedication of American Christians, smoking as they do, I am distressed. I cry right in my beer."

Of course many American Christians look on either smoking or drinking with displeasure. Still these legalisms tend to vary in their intensity in various geographical parts of the country. Evangelicals in Milwaukee who work in breweries may hold little objection to drinking but scorn the making or use of cigarettes. Those in the South who grow tobacco reciprocate by producing cigarettes and scorning the brewer's industry. In areas of the nation where neither are produced, both may be held in Christian contempt.

The Pharisees had developed a long list of laws which even included a hand-washing rule. No wonder Jesus said, "In vain they do worship me, teaching as doctrines the precepts of men" (Mk 7:7). With kosher sins it can be hard to tell exactly where the Word of God is supplanted by our own. For instance, the Bible commands us not to kill, commit adultery or steal. But the Pharisees' expanded list included provisions for hand washing, grain picking and blanket carrying that were just as serious to them.

Human requirements on top of God's requirements inevitably spell legalism. But the Bible delivers us from such contrived moral codes: we are to be judged on the basis of God's requirements alone. Paul says we should never allow others to judge us on the basis of their own legal code: "Let no one pass judgment on you in questions of food and drink" (Col 2:16). A positive Christian life is rarely achieved by exercising negatives: don't go to movies, don't dance, don't wear cosmetics and don't have any wine, even for your stomach's sake!

With all our preoccupation with the kosher, we seem to have ignored the fact that the sins of the mind are far more devastating. "Whatever goes into a man from outside [the type of food he eats] cannot defile him. . . . What comes out of a man is what defiles a man. For from within, out of the heart of man, come evil thoughts, fornication, theft, murder, adultery, coveting, wickedness, deceit, licentiousness, envy, slander, pride, foolishness" (Mk 7:18, 20-22). It is in the mind that we titillate ourselves with the possibility of evil. And it is in the mind that we grant ourselves permission for obvious and open transgressions. Yet seldom do we rebuke our impure hearts.

Since we cannot get caught at sinning in the mind, we do not stress those sins so heavily. And when we see someone involved in a kosher violation, we can say, "God, I thank thee that I am not like other men" (Lk 18:11). Usually this means we feel lucky to be discreet enough to not get caught.

All of us hope to live life free from discovery by Christian bloodhounds who snoop around to see how someone else's sin life is coming. There isn't a pastor alive who wouldn't trade his most vicious gossip for a congenial tippler if he could arrange the trade quietly.

Calling Up the Guard

Since sins of attitude are internal, they are difficult to control. To do so requires the toughness of the mind of Christ. Paul made some workable suggestions for this. In Colossians 3:15 he says, "Let the peace of Christ rule in your hearts." The word translated "rule" is also the word for "umpire." Like an official at a sporting event, the peace of God rules on the acceptability of every thought. Weak-minded Christians have not mastered the excellence of taking "every thought captive to obey Christ" (2 Cor 10:5). Rough mental discipline is unknown to permissive thinkers who will not submit to Christ as the referee of their minds.

Paul says in even stronger terms, "And the peace of God, which passes all understanding, will keep your hearts and your minds in Christ Jesus" (Phil 4:7). The word *keep* here could be translated "guard" or "garrison." To extend this word-picture a bit, think of a riot in a modern city. When the riot has grown so that it threatens the life of the city, the governor may call in the guard to restore order. The city could be said to be under garrison or guard. In the same way the peace of God should garrison our minds. God's spiritual authority will keep our minds open to only those things which are consistent with the dynamic mind. The garrison will not stop all thinking, only that which is against the will of Christ—just as the National Guard will not stop all commerce in the city, only those things which are against the welfare of the citizens.

Only by such toughmindedness can our minds be pleasing to God and productive for us, for "the thoughts of the wicked are an abomination to the LORD" (Prov 15:26). Again, the Scriptures teach that the wicked should forsake their ways, and the unrighteous their thoughts (Is 55:7).

Human gray matter, like human flesh, is weak. In his letters Paul contrasts two ways of thinking—with Christ and without. " 'For who has known the mind of the Lord so as to instruct him?' But we have the mind of Christ" (1 Cor 2:16). Arrogantly we can protest that we know how God ought to run the world (and our lives), or we can submit to him.

Jekyll and Hyde

If we try to operate by both minds, we may be trapped in what James calls double-mindedness. In a sense this resembles what George Orwell called doublethink: holding two conflicting ideas in our mind and accepting both. The mind of Christ is at peace with God while the carnal mind is at war with God; therefore, to try to accept the two contradictory minds is spiritual doublethink.

James then expands this with the words, "Cleanse your hands, you sinners, and purify your hearts, you men of double mind" (4:8). *Double-minded* could be correctly translated as "two-souled." If we try to live by both minds we will live in the hypocrisy of being two people at once. It is a kind of Jekyll-and-Hyde spirituality: a clumsy, Siamese-twin existence in which the spiritual is bound uselessly to the grotesque natural man.

Such an existence can never be a happy one. The two wills will ever battle each other. Purity and peace are cognates: the carnal mind is not pure and therefore it is not a mind at peace. Sören Kierkegaard wisely wrote, "Purity of heart is to will one thing." Peace is also to will one thing. This is the great gift of the dynamic mind.

The dynamic mind is also the end of the Christian neurotic. The word *neurosis* has been well defined for us by Paul Tournier.

The son who loves his father is right and healthy.

The son who hates his father is not right, but healthy.

The son who loves and hates his father at the same time is neurotic.

Neurosis rests upon an inner contradiction.[1]

Many Christians are not happy because an inner conflict is tearing them apart. This inner conflict is the quarrel between the old nature and the new. In receiving salvation we took on a new nature but kept a part of the old. And these two natures wrangle for supremacy on the battleground of our minds. Thus Paul exhorted the Ephesians, "Put off your old nature which belongs to your former manner of life and is corrupt through deceitful lusts, and be renewed in the spirit of your minds, and put on the new nature, created after the likeness of God in true righteousness and holiness" (4:22-24). Paul himself experienced this strange spiritual neurosis.

I don't understand myself at all, for I really want to do what is right, but I can't. I do what I don't want to—what I hate. I know perfectly well that what I am doing is wrong, and my bad conscience proves that I agree with these laws I am breaking. But I can't help myself, because I'm no longer doing it. It is sin inside me that is stronger than I am that makes me do these evil things. (Rom 7:15-17 LB)

This kind of spiritual conflict inevitably produces frustration and despair as well as some doubt about the value of our new life in Christ. But is this sort of neurosis an inescapable quandary? No. The mind of Christ, a part of the new man, supplies us with victory. "So you see how it is: my new life tells me to do right, but the old nature that is still inside me loves to sin. Oh, what a terrible predicament I'm in! Who will free me from my slavery to this deadly lower nature? Thank God! It has been done by Jesus Christ our Lord. He has set me free" (Rom 7:24-25 LB). We spiritual neurotics are delivered by the sole presidency of Jesus Christ, by the singular control of the mind of Christ.

When we have such dynamic minds, we are happy for two reasons. First, as I said before, there is no conflict in the single will. How wise is the familiar saying, "Let go and let God!" The most peaceless and tearing days of our lives are those when the old mind and the new struggle. The happiest are those when we let go and let God's singular will occupy our gray matter.

Second, happiness comes because the dynamic mind does not fear judgment. Do you remember the story of the man who could have had anything he wanted and merely asked for a copy of the *London Times* dated ten years ahead? There is a feeling that if we could have a secure future we could smile with greater regularity. This is the genius of the dynamic mind: our future is secured without threat. As the words of the hymn express it:

I don't know what the future holds,

But I know who holds the future.

Paul's happiness came as a result of that great guarantee. He would live not only forever, but forever beyond God's anger. "There is therefore now no condemnation for those who are in Christ Jesus" (Rom 8:1). Such is the hope that fuels the dynamic mind.

Thou art the way, the truth and the life.
Without the way, there is no going.
Without the truth, there is no knowing.
Without the life, there is no living.
Thomas à Kempis

[To his dying mother:]
I thank you for having given me life. When I think it through,
it has all been a single road to God.
St. Francis

Jesus loves me, this I know
For the Bible tells me so.
Anna B. Warner

6
Loving God

IN THE MUSICAL *Oliver,* Oliver Twist sings the haunting question, "Where is love?" Oliver's search is a universal search. And it is not merely love we search for but a steadfast and enduring love.

How often the fickle nature of human love disappoints us. After George Matheson, the hymn writer, found out he was going blind, he decided to tell his fiancée. He was crushed by her response. She gave back his ring and refused to be married to a man who would rapidly become dependent on her. From the bleak despair which claimed his mind after the engagement was broken, Matheson moved to new confidence in the Savior and wrote the hymn:

O Love that wilt not let me go,
I rest my weary soul in Thee;
I give Thee back the life I owe,
That in Thine ocean depths its flow
May richer, fuller be.

Matheson, in pain, made a discovery about the kinds and qualities of love. In the most shattering of circumstances we are often forced to leave the caprice of human love. Love is often frail and flies when faced with crisis.

The "Stuff" of God

God's love is different. His love is consistent and dependable. As Matheson learned, his love is there when other loves are gone. All other relationships have their source in his care.

Our happiness as Christians comes from this. The Scriptures do not read "God *has* love" as though love were a possession which God might lay aside in a grudge. Rather, the Bible says, "God *is* love" (1 Jn 4:8). Love is not an attribute of God but his substance and being.

We wouldn't say, "Man has protoplasm." Protoplasm is not something that we own and may lay aside if we wish. Rather, protoplasm is the very stuff we are made of. Destroy the "stuff" of man, and we cannot be. Just so, love is the "stuff" of God. God cannot exist without love.

I remember when I was cutting down a tree in our front yard and my four-year-old daughter, in wide-eyed wonder, was watching the chips fly as the axe chopped at the base of the trunk. She picked up one of the chips and said excitedly, "Daddy, I didn't know trees had wood in them." Trees, of course, do not contain wood. Trees *are* wood.

Love is the food of our spirit. We are nourished on it, or we are ill-nourished. God made us the way an engineer designs an engine, to run on a certain type of fuel. The only fuel designed to drive our spirits is God's infallible affection.

Abraham Maslow says we must have love and esteem before we can become self-actualized individuals, before we can become secure. So we all seek love that won't desert us when our needs are great. God's constant redeeming love is the source of our security and, therefore, of our happiness.

There for the Asking

Yet we have all struggled. We have all cried out to God and heard our cry ring like an echo in nothingness. It seemed that the heavens were brass, and we were alone. We ask, "Where is love?" convinced that God is absent. The love which is there is in reality not there until it is accepted.

Jesus told a parable of noblemen who refused to come to a banquet after having been invited. So the lame and blind were asked to come, and they did. For the poor who accepted it, love was abundantly there.

For years I knew about Niagara Falls. I knew that geographically it was tucked between the United States and Canada, shrouded in mist. But for me, it was not really there until I experienced it—until at last I stood there at the rain-soaked railing with my wife, lost in the reverie of the cascades.

It is not reasonable for us to ask non-Christians about the love of God. They may affirm it, but only theoretically. They will speak of it in secondhand quotes. Often we have precise words for defining such experience, precisely because we have not seen what we describe. If we had firsthand experience, the sheer joy would prevent our being able to define our ecstasy.

I remember, when my son and I took our first ride on a plane together, the excitement of his eyes seeking to drink in the experience. Earlier I had tried to tell him the emotion of it all and had failed. But at thirty thousand feet it didn't matter. Both of us felt what was too wondrous to define—flight! God's love cannot be known by definition. Theology can be a poor teacher if its instruction is a cold and academic mock-up of the real thing.

Some of us, however, lapse into unhappiness because we embrace a kind of spiritual masochism. Saved by the overwhelming presence of God's love, we turn with an inner feeling of incompleteness to ask, "Is this the love of God? Surely there must be something more. Can this be all?" With a kind of malcontent, we begin to search for deeper evidence of what we already possess. We are never more miserable than when we believe we have discovered God is inadequate to give us support because of the severity of our particular problems. Soon we may begin to castigate God for his failure to love us.

We are not so much problem solvers as problem seekers. Arriving at a state of utopia, we will do our utmost to create a problem just so we can "feel good." Even in the gadget-ridden completeness of Western civilization we rarely meet a happy person. Having everything, we still feel cheated. Deprived of big reasons to lament our sad estate, we take little grievances and magnify them. Viktor Frankl said it took him only a few days at Auschwitz to realize that he had never had a real problem in Vienna.

Even after we become Christians, we seem to want problems. Instead of drawing near to God, we retreat, like Jonah, from what we know to be his will. We want to love our world while fully aware that friendship with the world is enmity with God. As a result we make God remote. And when God grows remote, so does his love.

In our first coming to Christ, we exulted in the inner delight of his new presence. He filled us and then encircled us with love. Christ left no doubt that he was real and he was ours. What magnificent love! We had found the life beyond ourselves that filled the void within ourselves.

Then came the days of dread. Our confidence siphoned off into uncertainty. Pieter Geyl cries out for us our very anguish:

> The grace of God is gone.
> A vast indifference, deadlier than a curse,
> Chills our poor globe...[1]

In a cold room, the farther we are from the warmth of the fireplace, the less we feel its effect. Likewise, in the remoteness of our self-will, we feel the chill of our aloofness and shudder because we suppose he isn't there.

When we are redeemed, the indwelling Spirit of God convinces us that his love is there through the presence of Christ and will not forsake us even when we turn away from him. Consider the son who disobeyed his father and was sent to spend the night in the garret of their old house. The child was terrified to be alone amid the shadows and creaky darkness of the attic. But the father's own love moved him to compassion. While he could not commute the sentence, the father did climb to the attic to spend the night with his son.

God's love does not abandon us in the long night of our despair. We undergo trials. We endure long nights of crisis during our pilgrimage in this world, but we are never alone, for love has come to spend the night.

Paying for a Gift

God's love was costly, so costly it went to the cross to declare itself. But while his great love is not cheap, it is free. It is the gift of God. In fact, the root meaning of the word *grace* is "gift." Thus our happiness is destroyed not only when we create problems that don't exist, but also when we try to repay God for his magnificent love.

Any attempt to pay for any gift mars the gift itself. The gift becomes a purchase. If I offer you my watch as a gift, you have only to receive it to make it yours. But suppose I require some activity, like walking around the block, to make it yours. How have I altered the gift? You would be glad to earn so much by doing so little, yet in the very act of even such a small requirement the gift becomes a wage. The temptation is then to say, "Look how great a bargain I have made! I must be clever to have earned so easily something that is so valuable." The value of the Father's gift of life to us lies precisely in the fact that it cannot be bought.

Jesus alone is Savior! There is nothing we can add to grace. If there were, then in some minimal sense we would become responsible for our redemption. Any struggle to be a better person which aims at earning favor with God is a futile attempt to make payment to God for a completely free salvation.

A wise friend of mine once warned me that most of us are better at giving gifts than we are at receiving them. When we are given a valuable gift, a simple "thank you" never seems enough. We want to offer something in return—a kind of repayment. Our reluctance to receive God's grace illustrates this well. We want to contribute to grace for all it has done for us. The unfortunate consequence is that the love of God passes from gift to wage.

So much of our unhappiness comes from our attempt to purchase what is free. Protestants have long felt that Catholics cheapened grace by the sacrament of penance. Yet Protestants have a kind of penance of their own. Many feel that they must somehow deserve the gift of God. They will try to "do good" or "be especially earnest" or sentence themselves to reading the "begat" passages or withdraw their membership from civic clubs to devote their time to more spiritual pursuits. Often such activities are the result of their subconscious unwillingness to accept grace as a gift.

This Protestant penance might more aptly be labeled homemade atonement. If we thought about it, we would probably be less comfortable with the hymn "Amazing Grace" than with any other hymn. There are still thousands of believers whose good works are not so much a response to grace as an attempt to pay for it.

Such believers can at first know only a neurotic kind of discipleship. They cannot know acceptance with Christ nor ever really know true happiness. For happiness is never possible under the burden of heavy debt. Love is free in Christ, and we are best prepared to know happiness as the natural order of God's abundance when we accept it freely, with no attempts at self-atonement.

Infinite Love

By nature we are comfortable with limits and preciseness. I have known Christians who were miserable because they couldn't determine the exact quality of all their interpersonal relationships: Did Mr. A really like being an acquaintance? Would Mrs. B really stand by me in a crisis? Would Mr. C consider it presumptuous if I asked a personal favor?

Culturally we are children of ancient Rome, and we like organization and order. We like the dictionary. It gives us a certain word and then follows it by certain definitions that say, "These only may be the boundaries of this word: its meaning shall be no greater than these limits." Water, for instance, must be two parts hydrogen, one part oxygen; complete to the electron, we will not suffer it to be different. Then we go through life categorizing, organizing, defining, limiting, shelving, labeling and referencing every part of our experience.

I was amazed at the impertinence of Yuri Gagarin, the Soviet cosmonaut. On his primitive orbit of the earth he confirmed his atheism; since he did not find God in space, God must not exist. The illogic of looking for the light-year God within a few miles of earth never occurred to him. We cannot fly in a little corner of the cosmos and then make grand statements about a cosmoswide God. If we do not meet Moby Dick in the aquarium, shall we rule him out of the North Atlantic? Our categories are too shallow (not to mention our minds). Even when we aim our telescope at the night sky, we earthlings are still too nearsighted to see very far. While we can speak of God, let us confess that we are only microbes on a microscope slide, unable to imagine the existence of bacteriologists. The reality is too immense. God is bigger than our theology could ever define.

Infinite love? Infinity is a strange, uncomfortable dimension for us. Infinite being is God. Infinite time is eternity. Infinite knowledge is omniscience. Infinite power is omnipotence. Infinite existence is omnipresence. *Infinite love is agape.*

We discover misery only when we make God's love remote, for love is there. We are just as frustrated when we seek to earn his love, for his love is free. We will be equally miserable if we attempt to discover the limits of God's love, for it is infinite.

How frequently we illustrate the size of our guilt when we ask, "Would God love me if I committed such and such a sin?" The question is an attempt to make the infinite containable. We are like swimmers who are afraid our splashing will empty the ocean.

Guilt may cause us to put boundaries around God's love. It is as though we say, "My sin is too great to be absorbed by God's small love." We suspect that his love is somehow too small to really redeem us in the face of our gargantuan sins. What an indictment this accusation is to his limitless love! The Bible makes it clear that "as far as the east is from the west, so far does he remove our transgressions from us" (Ps 103:12).

Our false guilt is an effort to make things easier for God. But God wants us to trust our every burden to the buoyancy of his love. The acceptance of his great forgiveness is the best evidence of our complete surrender to him. We cannot really convince others of the trustworthiness of his love till we have committed all our sins to him, and never again dredge up the leftovers of our past.

Some years ago my family and I visited the Great Salt Lake in Utah. I remember reading about the superb buoyancy of the chemically saturated lake. Walking to the edge of the lake I noticed that far, far out in its waters were bathers at a great distance from the shore—too far, it seemed to me, to swim back in case of a crisis. Then I recalled the promise of chemistry: you cannot drown in these waters; they will not permit it. Only for a while did I linger near the shore. Soon I, too, was far out in the surf. And chemistry kept its promise. No crisis was possible.

Believers too frequently are distrustful of God's love and spend their lives in Christ splashing in the shallows. An ocean must be seen from the middle to know its vastness—so it is with God's love. And our joy will come as we quit seeking the limits of love and discover the thrill of its buoyancy.

The Mystery of Love

Last of all let us remember this: Love is the essence of Christian meaning, but its meaning is always imbedded in mystery. God's love is far above all human understanding. Like its existence, its constancy does not depend upon reason either.

When I was about nine years old, I received Christ as my Savior. I was immediately seized by the wonder of his love. I knew that God loved me, but was pained that I could find no reason for it. Unquestionably I was a sinner, and while at nine I could not be the same kind of sinner one finds in a cell block at San Quentin, I did know my sin was offensive to God and in some sense a barrier to the fullest appreciation of his love. I could not understand how his love could exist in spite of my sinful condition. I was also troubled about how a God who owned everything found my own love so essential to him.

In short, while God could exist without me, he seemed to need me. Yet I was the sole benefactor of our new love affair. In the illogic of our new relationship, I learned that a great quality of his love was the quality of mystery!

Our minds, however, hold little concord with anything which we can explain. A novel or a movie whose plot is obvious is dull. We will not work the same acrostic twice, and we scorn to play chess often with a weak opponent. Once we hold the key to unlock anything, our fascination with it is gone.

The intrigue of love is its glory! The mystery of divine emotion is that God cares intensely for us and yet we can't discover why. There is a strong and futuristic note in this mystery, for somewhere in the distant, unborn future is where this unsolvable love will have its glorious confirmation. Then earthly love and divine love will know all that can be known. The dark glass of human experience through which we have viewed life will be shattered. All question marks will be gone, and we will embrace God eternally in the full light of heaven.

To my wife:
Grow strong, my comrade ... that you may stand unshaken
when I fall; that I may know the shattered fragments
of my song will come at last to finer melody in you.
Will Durant, The Story of Philosophy

A thought transfixed me: for the first time in my life I saw
the truth as it is set into song by so many poets, proclaimed as
the final wisdom by so many thinkers. The truth—that
love is the ultimate and the highest goal to which man can
aspire. Then I grasped the meaning of the greatest secret that
human poetry and human thought and belief have to impart:
The salvation of man is through love and in love.
I understood how a man who has nothing left in this world
still may know bliss, be it only for a brief moment
in the contemplation of his beloved.
Viktor E. Frankl, Man's Search for Meaning

Let me not to the marriage of true minds admit impediment.
William Shakespeare

7
Loving Our Mates

ROMANCE IS AS OLD as Eve and moonlight. But Christians, until recent years, have talked only sparingly about it. For centuries, we talked freely of God's love but stingily of human love. It was not that boy-meets-girl affection was illegitimate, but rather that, because it was deemed so much less worthy than the love of Christ that it was not discussed.

In my teens, I generally thought that the devoted Christian family sat stiffly around the house reading Bible commentaries and talking "churchese." Human sexuality was thought of as antiseptic and liturgical, as proper as a baptismal formula or as diplomatic as a church board meeting. Romance—honest-to-goodness interpersonal affection—was not a matter of conversation among Christians. If there was such a thing as Christian romance, it was spiritualized with a grace so celestial it barely touched the ground. It inhibited itself in the name of being Christlike, and, forsaking every urge to snuggle, it preferred to simply shake hands.

If my views were wrong, they were not totally so. Sexual attraction may have been natural but in churches we spoke only of the supernatural. "Yes," we argued, "God put sexual love even in the life of Christians. But to speak of it is only to encourage it, and it is already too much the glutton. Sex overeats and is still hungry. Romance barely finishes dessert before it starts looking for the hors d'oeuvres again. Mentally it nibbles its way between meals, drooling over gourmet delicacies and forbidden fruit."

Now we openly discuss what only yesterday we ignored. We declare that there is nothing unchristian about sexuality. The love between a man and a woman is not a glandular snag in the fabric of spiritual maturity. To marry is to make our commitments firm before Christ and the courts, after which we may embrace in the full pleasures that God intended.

Next to divine love, romantic love is the most intimate and enduring kind. Most adults are moving into or have already entered marriage. But the high incidence of divorce and the abundance of marital counselors are evidence that not all is well. Statistics now prove that most marriages either end in divorce or leave the couple wistfully saying, "If I had it to do over again, I'd never marry the same person." Thus, while romantic love is universal, it is also a universal source of unhappiness.

The rate of divorce among Christians is also becoming alarming, though it is still less frequent than in society as a whole. There is some truth in the "pray together, stay together" cliché.

As in other relationships, in marriage complete happiness can result only when Christ is the center of the marriage. Still, Christian marriages, in spite of Christ, are sometimes lifelong prisons of unhappiness that keep marital love locked behind Christian hypocrisy.

Many couples, in the name of church doctrine or because of pride they could not surrender, will not admit that their relationship is sick. They keep their sinking marriages afloat for appearance's sake alone. They work their weary way toward their golden anniversaries, year by unhappy year. They quarrel up to the church steps on Sunday morning, then enter the service in an Academy Award performance of marital bliss. As their incompatibilities grow over the years, so does their acting ability. Finally, only the hardness of their eyes betrays their horrible struggle.

Were it not for the image such couples have to maintain in the church and the dependency of their children, they would likely shed their frustrating unions completely. However, unhappy Christian marriages can exist only when one or both believers apathetically pursue or ignore altogether the inner direction of Christ.

The Marriage of Eros and Agape

The common Greek word for human love is *eros*. The word is easy for us to understand because it was also the name of the Greek god of love whose Latin name was *Cupid*. Eros is the romantic affection out of which most marriages grow. Although the word *eros* is not found in the New Testament, the Bible does talk a great deal about marital love. It is a mystical yet a beautiful truth that the Bible dignifies romance by using the word *agape* (a word that usually connotes divine love).

In one sense the word *agape* is too lofty for the purely human relationship of a man and a woman. Still, it does say that a man's love for "his woman" (and vice versa) is to be characterized by the qualities of grace.

The greatest attribute of the love of God is that it does not require anything on our part to exist. A great passage like Romans 5 reminds us that God loved us "while we were yet sinners." Agape is Christ crying forgiveness above his executioners. God loves not only those who love him, but also those who will never love him. He loves those who crudely smudge his dignity with profanity or insult his holiness with indecency.

By contrast, eros cannot continue to give love unless its love is returned. There are many idealistic stories of human love thriving even in the face of great pain. But there are far fewer tales of a man who loved a woman who hated him or even ignored him for long periods of time.

In the counseling room I am discovering how fragile marital love is. It may be shattered by the slightest word or be lost by the turning of a head at the wrong time. Human love alone is not sturdy. The Bible still envisions marriage in Christ as God-like and uses agape (the infusion of divine happiness into human loving) to define it.

Let us remember that it is God's love which produced man. It was in that brief instant of time—while God's love for man existed and before romance was created—that man and God walked in Eden. But despite the perfect harmony between God and Adam, Adam was still alone. Animal by animal God brings to Adam the whole zoological kingdom, asking him to pick and name the consort to his being. But Genesis 2:20 laments that "there was not found a helper fit for him." Then during a deep sleep, God builds a woman from Adam's side, and when the creative amnesia is past, Adam awakes, beholds the shimmering creature beside him and says, "I have found my completion. . . . She shall be called woman, because she was taken out of man."

This story is told in Scripture from a masculine viewpoint. It begins with man as the original creation, finding a woman as a completion to himself. But the real meaning of the statement is that either sex is incomplete alone. Man completes woman in the same way that woman completes man.

The great issue of Eden was not just the creation of a man and a woman. The point was Adam's rib—symbolic of marital union. The intimacy of Adam and Eve's relationship is indicated in Mark 10:6-7: "Therefore a man leaves his father and his mother and cleaves to his wife, and they become one flesh." Marriage, from its beginning in Eden, is set above all other relationships.

God, however, did not give Adam and Eve the great gift of eros to set them free from their obligation to love him. They were still responsible to love God. Shortly after they sinned, God sought them out and reminded them of their obligation to love and obey him. Thus Adam and Eve discovered in Eden that romantic love which omits the love of God is a rocky course. The marriage which aims at happiness only on this purely human basis is likely headed for a lifetime of frustration.

As in other areas of serving Christ, happiness in marriage results from discipline. A proper marital relationship is not so much our goal as the result of the rightness of our primary relationship with God. Note the truth of Jesus' priority: "Seek first his kingdom and his righteousness, and all these things shall be yours as well" (Mt 6:33).

We have learned to fear the marital triangle as the symbol of a sick marriage. But three is a crowd only when the third person is human. When we make God the chaperone of our happiness, we can be confident in the outcome of our struggle toward marital maturity. To invite the Savior into our love is to return to Eden where God still walks with us and feeds us from the tree of abundant living. To shut Christ out is to be driven from the Garden and to live in tangleknots of neurotic suspicions and marriage for personal profit.

The same principle of self-surrender which leaves us open to spiritual happiness also leaves us open to marital joy. In a marriage where both partners insist on control, there is conflict.

Peace comes from submission. When I quit insisting that I must have things my way, God may use my life.

Several years ago I read about a couple with awesome incompatibilities. Each needed to drive; neither wanted to ride. The tedium of their togetherness had kept their home a raw nexus of exposed nerve ends. Their marriage became too burdensome to maintain. Finally they agreed to separate in preparation for divorce.

During the separation, Billy Graham came to their city for a crusade. On the same night, the husband and wife were both in the stands, each unaware that the other was at the service. While the invitation was being sung, the husband went forward to profess faith in Christ. The wife, who had been seated several thousand people away, also went forward. Before the altar they met, and having discovered God's love, they were able to begin rebuilding a badly eroded romantic love.

Neither Male nor Female

What about the issue of sexual role definitions? Are there biblical roles that are workable and flexible in the unstable sexual climate of our day?

Is there any credence in the statement that women are the weaker sex? Perhaps we should judge weakness as Will Rogers judged ignorance: "Everyone is ignorant, just in different areas!" Well, it is equally true that "everyone is weak, just in different areas." If we are talking of weightlifting or playing football for the Packers, then women may be weaker. If, on the other hand, we are talking about courage, love, wisdom, or competence in domestics or medicine or missions, they are not weaker.

The feminist belligerence in our day has been an unattractive front for the forces of liberation. Women, to establish their worth, have set new records in Sumo wrestling, long-distance running and cliff-diving at Acapulco. This athletic struggle has seized earnestly on traditionally masculine categories to advance the feminist cause. Similarly, any view of women's liberation is warped which promotes feminine independence at the expense of one's own sexuality. The word *woman,* it seems, has become incompatible with the word *mother* and has even begun to kick out the word *wife.*

When the Bible speaks of the submission of women, it does not operate under the fuzzy concepts held by many men and women. In Christ "there is neither Jew nor Greek, there is neither slave nor free, there is neither male nor female" (Gal 3:28). I think a good many ministers have in mind a picture of heaven in which most of those around the throne are men, the heroes of the faith. Such a notion is preposterous! The faith has many heroes, both male and female. As many women as men have served the cross both by the living of their lives and, in many cases, by giving their lives. In eternity there will be no differentiation, neither Jew nor Greek, slave nor free, male nor female.

Golda Meir was not permitted to touch the Holy Torah merely because her sex was wrong. I don't understand that. I do not approve of the old rabbinical prayer, "I thank God that I am not a dog, a Gentile, or a woman!" But even worse, as I grew up I never could understand why my denomination had churches that were gorged with women who remained separate and sometimes powerless in church. I have never been able to understand the contradiction of having twice as many women missionaries as men overseas, while at home women are treated as second-class citizens of the kingdom. The current conflicts over the status of women might be solved by remembering that men and women are—generally speaking—created to work in mutually supportive roles.

In Ephesians 5 and 6, Paul outlines the obligation of men,

women and children within the home. Children have the obligation of obeying their parents. Wives are generally asked to be submissive and husbands loving. Admittedly these are not concrete categories since in Ephesians 5:21 Paul says that all Christians—presumably even husbands and wives—are to submit to each other.

If the husband's responsibility in the relationship is to love, we must remember that at this point the metaphor that measures his love is Christ's love for the church. In essence, Christ so loved the church that he submitted himself to the utter offering of himself in love—the giving of his very life.

Such love completely destroys the artificial categories of the husband as monarch and the wife as subject. For the sacrificial love which Christ demonstrated on the cross will, in the life of a husband, cause him to give his very being to demonstrate his love at home. Utter love means utter submission. When we love we do not control but serve. No man has ever loved his wife that did not bend his masculinity till it could serve in joy the object of his love.

Certainly this passage never argues for the superiority of men. Whatever Paul is saying in Ephesians 5, he is not saying that men are better than women. He does seem to argue that men and women are created by God to fulfill different responsibilities in marriage. The gospel of Christ and its advancement is everybody's concern—men and women, all doing what they can to make the kingdom grow. This idea seems to indicate that in Christian ministry as in other secular areas of life, there are tasks which some of us perform better than others. The normal heterosexual union is the subject of Ephesians 5.

In passages like Romans 16:1-23, however, Paul demonstrates that women seem to perform better than men in many areas of church life. He gives tribute to at least eight women and their commendation always seems to be for the quality of their

Christian ministry. Women do have a natural inclination toward receptivity while men seem to be turned more toward an aggressive make-up. I think that the women's liberation movement has been shortsighted in overlooking this. It is not their argument for sexual equality that has bothered most, but their grasping for superiority in every area and structure of society.

I recognize that the idea of sexual roles will be distasteful to some who insist that the roles men and women play are only culturally imposed. These argue that there is nothing in either the physiology or psychology of men and women that confine them to lifestyles they have traditionally accepted. But to ignore the idea of roles leads to all sorts of difficulties. In contradiction to the conviction of some, I don't believe that women can play football as well as men. There is something to be said for men and women relating to society in ways that are consistent with their physical characteristics and sensitive make-up.

It is time we quit badgering the bachelor apostle Paul with anti-feminist cries. The issue of whether or not men are superior to women must be answered in many widely separate categories. Men are as superior to women in at least as many ways as they are inferior to women. Dorothy Sayers examines this question:

"A woman is as good as a man," is as meaningless as to say, ... "an elephant is as good as a racehorse"—it means nothing whatever until you add: "at doing what?" In a religious sense, no doubt, the Kaffir is as valuable in the eyes of God as a Frenchman—but the average Kaffir is probably less skilled in literary criticism than the average Frenchman, and the average Frenchman less skilled than the average Kaffir in tracking the spoor of big game. ... When we come to the elephant and the racehorse, we come down to bedrock physical differences—the elephant would make a poor showing in the Derby, and the unbeaten Eclipse himself would be speedily eclipsed by an elephant when it came to hauling logs.[1]

Submission and Response

In a similar way, the woman who is a good mother needs to understand that a part of what the Bible has to say about submission is in the interest of the best possible family life. In Ephesians 6:1-4 there are some excellent examples on the further roles of submission and response in the children that are to be raised in the home. The implication in these verses is that the mother who rebels against submission is going to have a hard time teaching submission to her children.

The whole issue of submission has nothing to do with superiority or inferiority of the sexes, but only the issue of relationship in marriage. Let us widen our perspective by remembering that the issues of submission and response are raised in a double metaphor of Christ and his church (Eph 5:22-31). In this passage it is impossible to separate the illustration of the body of Christ from the issue of marital union. Husbands and wives are to belong in oneness as inseparable as the union of Christ and his church. When this oneness is whole it is altogether pointless to argue for the control of either sex. The great truth is that marriage requires both. Just as one cannot have salvation without spiritual union with Christ, he cannot have a Christian home without the bond of one man and one woman.

At the risk of alienating woman-power advocates, I must give some attention to the concept of response in loving. Adam came into being as a response to God's love. God has ordained a rather similar role for women in relation to men. This is not to say that the husband is to provide all the vocational and emotional fireworks while the wife dutifully applauds and gapes with wonder at her husband's "godlike" achievements. Nor is it to say that women are only the cheering squad for the other half of the world, never contributing anything of their own.

Satan deceived Eve by saying, "Eat—and you will be like God" (Gen 3:5). Adam was bitten by the very same idea. Who would not rather own paradise than police it? But a throne has a seating capacity of only one. We are to respond to God's kingship in love, praise and adoration. Just as we live east of Eden because of our infatuation with our own status in life, marital paradise is lost in an egocentric approach to marriage.

Marital Eden is the home where the woman is fulfilled in her role of responder. If you are a woman, let it not be said that your station is inferior. Your right to dignity and respect and even career is guaranteed by Scripture. Your designation as "helper" does not mean "slave." Your husband is to love you as Christ loved his church. Your response as his wife is to be subject to your husband and see that you revere him.

The greatest of all passages on feminine response is Proverbs 31:10-31. Here is a picture of a woman who magnifies and honors her husband and her home. The Scripture comments, "The heart of her husband trusts in her, and he will have no lack of gain" (v. 11).

This passage sees initiation and response in their proper roles as the ingredients of a stable marriage. It does not follow Ogden Nash's suggestion that every marriage needs a little "incompatibility" as long as the husband has the "income" and the wife is "pattable."

Shakespeare built in biblical categories in *The Taming of the Shrew* when he had Katherine say to the ladies of Senor Baptista's house:

Thy husband is thy lord, thy life, thy keeper,
Thy head, thy sovereign; one that cares for thee,
And for thy maintenance commits his body. . . .
Such duty as the subject owes the prince

Even such a woman oweth to her husband;
And when she is froward, peevish, sullen, sour,
And not obedient to his honest will,
What is she but a foul contending rebel,
And graceless traitor to her loving lord?
I am ashamed that women are so simple
To offer war where they should kneel for peace;
Or seek for rule, supremacy and sway,
When they are bound to serve, love and obey.[2]

If you mix the roles of initiation and response in marriage, unhappiness usually follows. If a woman usurps the role of initiator, then a man has only two possible paths open to him. He may quietly (or noisily) accept the role of responder. The only other path is to allow the union to decay.

Submission in the New Testament is not sexually determined. Ephesians 5:21 makes it clear submission is for both men and women: "Be subject to one another out of reverence for Christ." Paul teaches in Philippians 2 that all Christians are to have the mind of Christ and surrender arrogance in a spirit of submission to Christ. Only Christ is great, and all Christians, regardless of sex, should bow their heads before their Master and Lord.

The husband, nonetheless, is to lead his wife and family as he can, preparing the soil of spirituality for a harvest of good relationships. 1 Corinthians 11:3 suggests that God is the head of Christ as Christ is the head of man, and the man is the head of the woman. This is not a chain of command for ordering life but a chain of relationships by which God participates in a full way in family life.

Nowhere is the understanding of initiation and response more imperative in Christian marriage than in the area of sexuality. It is refreshing in the current sexual revolution to see Christians discussing sexuality with objectivity and openness.

Where the Bible comments on Christian sexuality, it sees it as a response to human love and never as a substitute for it.

The sex drive, according to many Bible passages, is to be given free expression in marriage. Consider Proverbs 5:15-19: "Drink water from your own cistern, flowing water from your own well" (v. 15). Permissiveness and extramarital sex are prohibited.

"Let thy fountains be dispersed abroad, and rivers of waters in the streets" (v. 16 KJV). Sexual expressiveness should have complete freedom within marriage. Sexual stinginess is never advocated here by the Scripture.

"Let your fountain be blessed, and rejoice in the wife of your youth" (v. 18). This refers to the rapture and joy that comes from climactic sex. The phrase "wife of your youth," found in several other places in Scripture, indicates that a man is never to share sex with anyone other than the person he married when he was young, even though in the later years of the marriage his spouse may not be as endowed with physical beauty as she was when they were both young.

"Let her be as the loving hind and pleasant doe; let her breasts satisfy thee at all times; and be thou ravished always with her love" (v. 19 KJV). Again liberality in sexual relationships is emphasized, and the pleasantness of sexual foreplay is suggested.

Many passages, like this one, deal openly with the importance and beauty of Christian sex. One remembers the Rev. Mr. Bowdler who went through Shakespeare's plays and expunged all mention of sex in some weird attempt to "Christianize" them. Had Mr. Bowdler applied his principle to the candid passages of the Bible dealing with marital sex, the Scriptures themselves would have been impoverished.

The sexuality taught by the Scriptures is as clear as it is practical. A woman I heard of confessed a problem to her pastor that was having a drastic effect on her home—frigidity. 1 Corinthians 7:4 teaches that a wife's body belongs to her husband. The woman suddenly felt as though she had wronged her mate. In the next few weeks, her sexual stinginess was cleansed and the marital relationship restored.

In the same way a husband's body belongs to his wife. Thus no man is permitted to have an extramarital affair nor even a flirtatious fantasy. Men perhaps need to work harder than women at guarding the portals of their imagination so their minds will lead their bodies in maintaining their marriages.

Not by Sex Alone
Notwithstanding the beautiful dimension of marital sex mentioned in such passages as Hebrews 13, we may forget that sexuality will always prove inadequate as the sole basis for Christian marriage. The real happiness of the relationship calls for a much deeper bond than this.

Keeping sexuality in its place is very difficult. Movies, novels and billboards make us feel it is the *sine qua non* of marriage. Sex stands for love instead of its being a response to love. The error of *sexus maximus* which C. S. Lewis commented on.

Yes, I think there is lots to be said for being no longer young: And I do most heartily agree that it is just as well to be past the age when one expects or desires to attract the other sex. It's natural enough in our species, as in others, that the young birds should show off their plumage—in the mating season. But the trouble in the modern world is that there is a tendency to rush all the birds on to that age as soon as possible and keep them there as long as possible, thus losing all the real value of the other parts of life in a senseless, pitiful attempt to prolong what, after all, is neither its wisest, its happiest or most innocent period. I suspect merely commercial motives are behind it all; for it is at the showing off age

that birds of both sexes have the least sales resistance.[3]
Paul Tournier quotes a psychologist who compared human loving to the theater: Love for the woman is itself the drama; for man it is the intermission.[4] Perhaps these basic and divergent understandings of love between the sexes say that sexual rapport by itself is not enough to produce marital happiness. There must be mutual interest and friendship.

Although there is some truth in the phrase "opposites attract," a healthy union is fostered by a communion of interests. In a recent counseling session with a couple, I became aware of the significance of this principle. Their marital problems indicated they were victimized by divergent interests. He was impeccably neat; he liked rising at six o'clock in the morning and jogging two miles before breakfast; he liked tennis and calisthenic programs; he disliked cocktail parties, only tolerating them in the name of marital congeniality.

Everywhere he was left, his wife was right. She liked to sleep late, loved parties, hated sports and was imprecise with her housekeeping. The only thing they seemed to love together was spaghetti and breadsticks. Admittedly that was not much of a start, but beginning with spaghetti and breadsticks, they are trying to develop some common interests which, at this point, are so crucial to their marriage.

These diverse interests may take permanent forms. Screwtape's advice to Wormwood was to seek to undermine relationships by widening the interest gap and playing upon the pet peeves. "When two humans have lived together for many years, it usually happens that each has tones of voice and expressions of face which are almost unenduringly irritating to the other. Work on that. Bring fully into the consciousness of your patient that particular line of his mother's eyebrows which he learned to dislike in the nursery, and let him think how much he dislikes it."[5]

Just as differences alienate, common interests weld. The presence of Christ in the marriage will permit us to overlook the offenses while we magnify the graces of our mates. "Forgive us our debts, as we forgive our debtors" is the redeeming principle of forgiveness in Christian marriage. Christians who reflect on God's forgiveness of all their sins can find a tolerance for their mates' annoyances and faults.

The common interests that make for marital happiness are not, however, such activities as mixed golf leagues, movie viewing or Christmas shopping. Neither are they the rituals that every home must perform day by day, unexciting occupations such as setting alarm clocks, feeding pets, washing dishes. Such things occupy much of the conversation that flows between married couples. And when only conversation about these kinds of activities occurs, the marriage may die by default. Where the conversation is weak, so is the marriage.

The key is the word *being*. This means more than existence. It implies self-awareness and conscious reflection. Marriage is not the symbiotic tie between two automatons, one of which agrees to wash the dishes while the other mows the lawn. It is the vow of two who promise love, honor and ultimate concern in sickness and health. How utterly tragic that following these commitments, the relationship may degenerate into mundane routine and perfunctory dialog. How utterly correct was Dr. Maltarello when he said that "an illness which is widespread in modern times, is the absence of inwardness."[6] But the "absence of inwardness" is eliminated in the truly Christian marriage.

Christ himself is the abundance of inwardness—the "being" filler. At the moment of salvation he moves inward and indwells us forever. Christ in our lives is the hope of glory. This affects not only the mission of the church but also the meaning in our marriages. The Scriptures literally abound with a testimony to the "abundance of inwardness" that is in Christ.

"Christ may dwell in your hearts through faith" (Eph 3:17). "You are God's temple and . . . God's Spirit dwells in you" (1 Cor 3:16). "If we love one another, God abides in us" (1 Jn 4:12). His indwelling word is responsible for the quality of our inwardness. That is why the Bible says, "Let the word of Christ dwell in you richly" (Col 3:16).

The depths of spiritual inwardness within marriage is a well-spring never exhausted. Moment by moment it draws on the fullness of the Spirit, and day by day it provides fascination and depth. It was said of the manna that it was fresh every morning (Ex 16:21). Like the manna, a happy marriage is the gift of God, and those who achieve it will say regularly throughout the passing years, "Thank you, Father, for the fullness of being that comes from life in Christ. Thank you that it is fresh every morning."

The universe, which is not merely the stars and the moon and the planets, flowers, grass, and trees, but other people, has evolved no terms for your existence, has made no room for you, and if love will not swing wide the gates, no other power will or can.
James Baldwin, The Fire Next Time

These were men and women of a new type. They had faith, a holy faith, in the new ideals of man.
Svetlana Alliluyeva

No man is an Island, entire of itself. . . . Any man's death diminishes me, because I am involved in Mankind; and therefore never send to know for whom the bell tolls; it tolls for thee.
John Donne

8
Loving
Our World

I HAVE BEEN a Christian long enough to see that churches are often communication jams. There is too much talking and too little listening. Sometimes churches are sterile places where people meet and shake hands with their mittens on. The late Father Divine once criticized the clergy with the words, "too many of us 'meta-physicians' have forgotten how to 'tangibilitate.' " The question is hard: Do we know how to relate to others in the church? Or are we afraid to touch? Do we really trust our brothers?

During a youth retreat, the young people of our church once played an interesting game. They stood in a circle, blindfolded, and placed some member of the group in the center of the ring. Then they asked him to "fall in faith" and trust that he would be caught by other members of the group. The whole exercise was to demonstrate how dependable we actually felt others were. While most agreed that these were the best friends they had on this earth, they were unable to let themselves fall in the confidence that they would be caught.

Love is the goal of all our relationships. "If we love one another, God abides in us and his love is perfected in us" (1 Jn 4:12). The verse is a pointblank accusation of the hypocrisy in most of our relationships. Our claim to know God's love is empty unless we love. Love as portrayed in 1 Corinthians 13 is all sounding brass and tinkling cymbal without a continual demonstration on the sidewalks and in the shops. This is the love that must reach around the world.

A World to Love

How wide our love must reach! In the heart of every true believer is born a new concern for the people of our world—the hungry and the lonely, near and far. Christians everywhere are beginning to ask what the widest implications of Christian ministry are. Jesus loves widely, and if we have not seen the Savior in love with the whole world, we have not seen the whole Savior.

Fifty years ago social gospelism criticized the church for trying to feed the hungry rather than trying to preach an eternal gospel. Some liberation theologians may be going too far in our day, but they are an indication that many Christians once again are crying out for a new worldwide concern. We have seen enough of bourgeois Christians who have emphasized orthodoxy while enjoying the cherries and cream of Western economies. Third World countries have looked at overweight Christians in the West and have condemned us for treasuring our comfortable conservatism more than Christian compassion.

Here and there are noble voices calling us to a new world-consciousness. Their voices are weak and often lost among the wealthy young musicians and lecturers who have found Christian entertainment and education lucrative and fun regardless of whatever else may be happening in the world. Even churches which have become close-knit and caring families to their own members have not looked beyond their walls where ignorance and hunger are relentless killers.

New video churches are taking an amazing rake-off of funds to pay network contracts and broadcast expenses. Their greatest use of media income seems to be the building of large, expensive studios and the purchase of personal airplanes to transport the "stars" here and there to be adored in coliseum worship services.

One of the greatest gospel television magnates was asked why he insisted on building such a large and expensive church building when there were so many poor in the world. He confessed that if he were to use building funds to feed the poor, the poor would only eat the food and would then be hungry again; having spent all on the poor, he would still not have a church building. Eight of the largest video evangelists together collected nearly a billion dollars in a single year. Yet their world concern was almost negligible.

Only here and there does one see such remarkable compassion as that shown by Mother Teresa of Calcutta or Ron Sider of the United States. But wherever such admirable souls are found, we hear the message that Western Christians have lost their way in the egoistic indulgence of their own shallow concerns.

The true gospel is a constant reminder that people everywhere are important to God. The current myopia that causes us to see only our own little needs is a denial of the Christ whose final act on this globe was to send out his church to teach, baptize and heal.

The church needs to cry to her overweight constituency to

lift up their eyes to behold the emaciated lovers of God who wait to be fed. Ears must be unstopped to hear the whimpering Third World children crying for hunger and education.

Let us not presume any longer that there is a kind of honest discipleship that would train Christians to know and to serve God only on an American level. God cannot be served until, like true ministers of Christ, the church puts on its seven-league boots and steps across the ocean to minister to those who have never yet beheld a credible Western minister coming with bread and truth, sharing both light and care.

In the meantime, let us quit speaking of discipleship only as a classroom project where we learn to fill in Bible worksheets that provide us an academic understanding of God or ethics. To be a disciple is to care about the whole world at once as Jesus cared. To be a disciple is to reach out to the hungry and those in prison and to weep as the Savior wept over the lostness of a world hungry for bread and meaning. We cannot be disciples until we have so imitated our Teacher.

Emerging from Hibernation

Christians are to love vertically—to God. But we are to love laterally too. We find people of different colors, different languages, different religions, different intelligence, different social position, different sex, different politics and different wealth throughout the world. But we are given only one assignment—to love! We are to love every name on the world census. We are to love close and far away: countrywide and internationally. We are to love the "good guys and the bad guys," our friends and God's friends. And unless we express that love, there is reason to doubt whether we actually do love. As Shakespeare wrote in *Two Gentlemen of Verona,* "He does not love who does not show his love."

St. Francis, in forsaking self, fell in love with everything God had made—the universe itself. He preached to the birds, for he saw them as God's little sisters. He called the sun his brother and the moon his sister. He saw every person as special. Even the feeble-minded were his peers. Bullies could not intimidate him, for however they brutalized him, they were yet the special friends of God.

I am not sure how he managed this love, but I suspect it was because he did not overlove himself. He had crucified Francis and reckoned him dead. And when Francis was on the cross, his body (whom he called Brother Ass) became the vehicle for his heavenly Father to magnify himself. Francis did not despise himself, because he knew that God had created him. But it seemed to Francis that his own flesh was a cheap vehicle for the Father to use.

Francis was often alone, but he was not a recluse. He confidently walked in communion with his world. He used the world as the only arena he had to strengthen his relationship with God. We are afraid to go into our world for fear that we will lose our relationship with God there. We leave our prayer closet and quake before a hostile environment. We feel that if it were possible for us to withdraw from all human affairs, our problems with the world would be solved.

Alas, we must emerge from hibernation! We bang elbows with people on the crowded sidewalks; a rude motorist shouts an obscenity; a store clerk ignores us when we are hurried and frustrated. And somehow in the press the question must come: "How, Father, do you love mankind?" (The irony is that we are a part of the humanity we wonder how God can love.) And sometimes when we consider the long and senseless inhumane history of man, we ask, "Why do you love mankind?" But grace is the essence of God's love and his love never has to answer how or why. God loves others for exactly the same reason that he loves us: it is his nature to love.

The Problem with Brother-loving

But it is not *our* nature to love. The power for loving others must be given to us by Christ. Another irony is that the obscene motorist or the apathetic clerk are not necessarily the most difficult people for us to love. Their nature can be excused many times because they are outside the fellowship of the church. Often, loving others is most difficult with fellow believers. *Philadelphia* is the problem. The word *philadelphia* appears five times in the New Testament and is usually translated "brotherly love" or "brotherly affection," always referring to love between Christians. Romans 12:10 states, "Love one another with *philadelphia.*" 1 Thessalonians 4:9 requires, "But concerning *philadelphia* you have no need to have anyone write to you, for you yourselves have been taught by God to love one another." Hebrews 13:1 says, "Let *philadelphia* continue." 1 Peter 1:22 commends "sincere *philadelphia,*" and 2 Peter 1:7 enjoins us to supplement "godliness with *philadelphia.*" Despite these exhortations, we are all too often struck dumb that those who claim to know God's truth and who say they have experienced grace seem so unlike Christ (and ourselves). Many of us have walked out on the "two-faced fellowship" never to return. Having been astounded at the majestic quality of God's love, we wonder how Christ could look out over humanity with such great forgiveness. How will we ever learn to love everybody?

As we think about Will Rogers's words, "I never met a man I didn't like," we wonder if Will ever got out much. Perhaps he had never been to a church board meeting. Would Will have felt that way had he met Adolf Hitler or Caligula or Brother Fuddy-Duddy? But even shallow generalities like Will's are preferable to the phony show Christians enact. We sing warmly of the love of God and smile through gritted teeth in the church. We pretend to love all the brethren, but our pretense is not the *philadelphia* which God has ordered for his church.

Consider for a moment the two words *like* and *love*. Will Rogers used the former, but the Bible uses the latter. When I first read Joseph Fletcher's definition of love, I thought for a while all my conflicts were solved. Fletcher believes that to love someone is to will for them the best set of circumstances that can be theirs. Fletcher didn't say you had to like everyone—only love them. I felt liberated!

I could not remember one person who was so distasteful that I hoped he or she would be victimized. Most of the time I was able to wish him or her a wonderful life, filled with good things—and one that would never require us to say "Good day." I could still hold negative attitudes. When I saw unlikable persons at a distance I would think, "I wish you the best possible circumstances, but please don't bother me." I was like Tevye's rabbi's blessing on the Czar, "May the Lord bless and keep the Czar . . . far away from us." We, too, are willing for God to bless our foes, but only at a distance.

Christians state glibly that they love the whole world, while they permit themselves animosities within their immediate world. World love is a philosophical credo. But loving the world at large can only be done by loving face to face the world that is not so distant. It is foolish to say we love humanity; it's people we can't stand.

The truth is, of course, real love must abandon sweeping philosophy in favor of the intimate. The only real love is point blank. Real *philadelphia* is positive. It looks at self first rather than at others. We tend to be quite forgiving of our own mistakes and foibles. But we tighten our requirements considerably for what is acceptable behavior in others. Their sins are far more despicable than the same offenses are for us.

We also know how to make use of all our relationships and yet ever justify it. How difficult it is to reward even our dearest friends without some ulterior motives. Subconsciously we list beside the names of our friends the fringe benefits of the relationships. "Bill is the dearest friend I have." (He also helps with my plumbing problems from time to time.) "Sue is a marvelous friend." (And our volunteer babysitter.)

The idea of profit and friendship strikes most poignantly when some member leaves our church and joins another. I hear statements like, "I'm sure going to miss old brother so-and-so. (Besides, he is a tither, and we're not replacing all these tithers that we're losing.)" Or when an impressive citizen visits the church, there are usually remarks like, "Pastor, we've got to try to get Mr. A. in our church; he's a wonderful man (and quite active in city politics, I understand)."

Although James 2:1-5 warns against grading church visitors according to status, we somehow gratify our egos by keeping a tally on the profits and losses of our friendships. Unquestionably the size of our own egos varies proportionately with the supposed importance of those we encounter.

There is absolutely no profit for God in any of his relationships with us. The profit is on our side. We bring nothing into our affair with him, yet he supplies everything. Our love would be most like God's if we were to search for the most unprofitable, unlovely person in the world and try to cultivate a warm and beautiful friendship.

A man once wrote Bishop Fulton Sheen that he was contemplating suicide. He was young but tragically deformed. The disease which had crippled his body had ravaged his nervous system, and his spastic movements left him nearly incommunicado with the rest of society who drew back from him and left him victimized by loneliness.

But Bishop Sheen invited him to lunch, and they became acquainted. Sheen apparently did not notice his deformities nor his incessant drooling during the meal. After several visits together, a friendship was created, and all thoughts of suicide were abandoned by the boy. He found new meaning in life because he had been loved by someone quite unlike himself.

Vengeance Is

Vengeance, unfortunately, is a barrier between saving love and brotherly love. Some ancient civilizations had a law that has been referred to as *lex talionis,* or the law of retaliation. Because of the basic human instinct of self-preservation, the law was a natural way of trying to establish justice. If someone was wronged, it was only fair that the culprit be apprehended and punished officially with the same kind of wrong he had inflicted. Exodus 21:23-25 reflects the Jewish understanding of this eye-for-an-eye justice.

While this idea of vengeance was an improvement on other ancient systems which allowed far excessive vengeance, nonetheless, *lex talionis* is not for believers. Even though it is a part of our nature, it is beneath our dignity, for we have received the Father's love. As we have received love we did not deserve, we must give our love the same way.

Zoo animals have been known to bite themselves in vicious mutilation when they were unable to get at their enemies through the bars. Every grudge we allow to exist side by side with saving love is self-destructive, eating away our psyches. One authority even suggested that nobody ever tried to kill himself unless he wanted some other person to die.

Few Christians bring such strident vengeance against their brothers. But even the most mature of us may have tantrums of resentment toward others. We may jab with cutting gossip, or we may indulge in self-pity. We rarely say, "I'll eat a worm and then I'll die," but we have been known to say, "If my church doesn't appreciate me, I'll join another." Hebrews 12:15 warns us about the destructive quality of holding grudges. No root of bitterness should be allowed to penetrate our lives.

This picture from Hebrews is graphic. Trees stay firmly planted in the ground, despite great winds, because of their extensive root systems. If, however, these roots become diseased and rot, the tree loses its anchor. Likewise, bitterness (though hidden deep under the surface) can ultimately bring about our downfall. Grudges defile the kingdom and deny the church's claims to love the world.

One final kind of vengeance also operates in the fellowship. I call this the *miniresentment*. Often in the press of close living, we don't have much "hate time," so it seems we must have flashes of resentment, as perhaps when a motorist crowds us in rush-hour traffic. Since all the discipline of mind and muscle must be directed to the traffic, we may only flash like a computer being fed a mutilated card and continue on in our lane of frenzied autos.

But no vengeance, whether it manifests itself in murder or miniresentment, is permitted in the brotherhood. Paul's words are wise indeed: "Beloved, never avenge yourselves, but leave it to the wrath of God; for it is written, 'Vengeance is mine, I will repay, says the Lord'" (Rom 12:19). When Matthew 5:44 counsels us to love our enemies, what it is really saying is "Wipe out your enemies with love." If Jesus could not permit James and John to call down fire on the inhospitable Samaritans, neither will he permit us to set aside our love of our world for even a moment of hatred.

Hatred is as great a sin as any other. Miniresentments are merely hatred in embryonic form. Just as gluttony and drunkenness separate us from God, hatred is a terribly destructive, mental-attitude sin (one of those sins we can't get caught at). Hatred belongs to our past (Tit 3:3). We are to have the mind of Christ and rebuke malice, envy and all mental-attitude sins, and to love widely in our world.

Such sins isolate believers. They break our fellowship. For

Cain, murder was merely the furthest extension of the screaming silence that passed between him and his brother. Then Abel was bludgeoned by Cain's unrestrained grudge. No doubt when some little resentment first separated Cain and God, he allowed envy to shut him off from God; soon it shut him off from his brother as well. Only as we are in complete fellowship with our brother may we claim fellowship with God. Remember, "If any one says, 'I love God,' and hates his brother, he is a liar" (1 Jn 4:20).

How often our churches are notoriously unhappy places because we are not on speaking terms with one another. The problem, of course, is that we are not on speaking terms with God. The only solution is to seek the Spirit's ministry so our rapport with God leaves us fully open to each other. Then our world will quit asking us for some other indication of our allegiance to God. "By this all men will know that you are my disciples, if you have love for one another" (Jn 13:35).

But where was I to start? The world is so vast, I shall start with the country I know best, my own. But my country is so very large. I had better start with my town. But my town, too, is large. I had best start with my street. No: my home. No: my family. Never mind, I shall start with myself.
Elie Wiesel, Souls on Fire

If you see yourself as a part of Christ, you will act like Christ; if you see yourself as fallen Adam, you will act like fallen Adam. We act out our perceived identities.
Peter J. Kreeft, Heaven: The Heart's Deepest Longing

You took the good things for granted—now you must earn them again. For every right that you cherish, you have a duty which you must fulfill. For every hope that you entertain, you have a task that you must perform. For every good that you wish to preserve, you will have to sacrifice your comfort and your ease. There is nothing for nothing any longer.
George Washington

9
Ministers with Christ

THE WORD *MINISTER* has become a clerical-collar word that most believers never apply the term to themselves—it seems too grand for ordinary, unordained believers. But the exact opposite is true! *Ministry* is not a professional word. It is one of humility which Christ applied to himself. It speaks of the joy that goes with us as we obey Christ to minister to a world in need.

Ministry is a term of caring and loving. It is a word for others, a word that liberates us from ourselves, a sculpting word to fashion us into the image of Christ who "came not to be ministered unto, but to minister, and to give his life a ransom for many" (Mt 20:28 KJV). Ministry is a giving of our lives. It is an extension of the Incarnation. As Jesus came in the fullness of God, we must go out to serve in the fullness of Christ.

All great ministers find that giving their lives for others brings them to a cross. Actually, they live crucified lives, for crucifixion is the process and not the goal for all who would be ministers.

How shallow we are to believe that singing hymns can substitute for the direct command to serve God in our world. We define worship as service when we speak of worship services. But ministry holds the dynamic dimension of risk beyond the sanctuary. Worshipers live too much indoors. Servants walk in the world beyond liturgy and candled assemblies.

The search for servants is the great obsession of the Holy Spirit as it was of the Son of God himself when he walked the earth. "Follow me," he cried to the fishermen, "and I will make you become fishers of men" (Mk 1:17). The world was in desperate need of salvation, and Jesus' ministry was to rescue this beleaguered planet. But his plan included us, and so Christ spent his ministry on earth looking for servants who were willing to join him in his vast rescue operation.

He preached to the dispossessed throngs, but he found only a few who would minister with him. "Many are called, but few are chosen," he said (Mt 22:14). He knew that most of those who heard him would, like the rich young ruler, only say, "Thanks, but no thanks!" But here and there he met men and women whose lives were changed by his love. These saw their very lives as payment for a debt they acquired when Christ became their Lord. Willingly, these would offer him their entire being.

They were amazed to discover that their ministry did not require exceptional talent, only the generous giving of self. Those who did give found they not only walked in the center of love but also acquired a new identity with Christ. As servants they willingly and joyfully give away the prized personal freedom. They give it to Christ just as Christ gave it to the Father.

Perhaps the issue of surrender sets our own decision making too much in the middle. Do we have any right to act as though we have surrendered the prize of our own lives when all that has worth in our lives has already been purchased at the expense of Christ's own sacrifice? We have been bought. Simon Peter spoke of our purchase when he said, "You know that you were ransomed from the futile ways inherited from your fathers, not with perishable things such as silver or gold, but with the precious blood of Christ, like that of a lamb without blemish or spot" (1 Pet 1:18-19). Having no right to ourselves, we still protest the surrender of our lives to ministry. We fight with the Almighty, lest our little agendas be given over to something great.

The decision to be a servant still lies within our own will. God does not force us to take steps for him that we have not already agreed are important to us and represent the direct desires of our own lives. At last we see the tremendous obligation of our surrender. God may allow the entire circle of our friends to be lost forever if we do not allow him to use us to bring them to faith. At the risk of losing the entire earth, therefore, God waits for us to serve. If indeed he does own us, there is nothing unreasonable that God can ask us to do. To minister is to participate in God's redeeming plan.

In the book of Exodus God begins a rescue operation through ordinary people. Here at the dawn of Hebrew history, there are three million aching people, all beloved by God and at the same time the victims and slaves of one of the most anti-Semitic governments the world has known. Israel's plight in Egypt is the story of cutbacks and infanticides and executions. It is the saga of children branded with the chattel markings of the tyrannical emperor they served.

Rescuing these Jewish slaves was a big task! The operation called for tremendous personal hardship and the utmost in courage. God searched out a man who would serve him. But he was not unreasonable to Moses. He owned Moses. Was what God asked unfair? Was Moses free to disallow what God wanted? Moses reluctantly did obey. He was slow in learning to accept what the all-knowing God asked of him.

The Call to Compassion

God knew the tale of human injustice. Perhaps the bitter cry of the writer of Ecclesiastes describes the thoughts of the Holy God we serve.

> Again I saw all the oppressions that are practiced under the sun. And behold, the tears of the oppressed, and they had no one to comfort them! On the side of their oppressors there was power, and there was no one to comfort them. And I thought the dead who are already dead more fortunate than the living who are alive; but better than both is he who has not yet been, and has not seen the evil deeds that are done under the sun. (Eccles 4:1-3)

The injustice of this world always touches God. And his concern touches the world with ministry. And for every ministry there is a minister whose heart yearns for the very things God cares for. When our surrender to God knows no unreasonable demands, we enter a dynamic union with Christ. As Paul once said, "For his sake I have suffered the loss of all things . . . that I may know him and the power of his resurrection, and may share his sufferings, becoming like him in his death, that if possible I may attain the resurrection from the dead" (Phil 3:10). And elsewhere he urged the Romans to "present your bodies a living sacrifice, holy, acceptable unto God, which is your reasonable service" (Rom 12:1 KJV).

Out of this identity with Christ true ministry is born, for when we are one with Christ, we begin to glorify the Father as he did. We begin to be moved with compassion as he was moved. And we cannot read of the ministry of Christ without seeing this word *compassion*. The Bible uses it to mean the inward grip of the stomach, a yearning to identify with those who suffer and to offer them comfort, care and a hope for the future.

The great men and women of modern missions were moved with compassion for the destitute, ignorant and downtrodden of the world. Their care and their identity in Christ caused them to yearn restlessly to please their Savior who also hears the crying of those who need the touch of God. He is a listening God, and when we have given our lives to him, we will be listening servants.

A friend of mine was thirteen years old at the time of the Nigerian Civil War with the secessionist Katanga province. Even at that young age he was in the army, and he was wounded by a grenade. He barely survived. The crisis of war left him aching. Even now he is a mass of scars. Thus the ugly question raises its head—"Does God know about this?"

The New Testament is a book full of evidence that God hears the suffering. On Olivet Jesus commissioned his church to spend her life in ministry. He called her to enter the world preaching so that all might be saved. God hears the cries of those living and dying without Christ. The church is therefore sent to the same dramatic task to which God sent Jesus.

But our radical call to service is poorly understood. Most of us join a church to enhance our reputations or bring respectability to our lifestyles. It has seldom occurred to us that we have not been called to be recipients of glory but to be ministers. We in the West have developed lives of self-aggrandizement. Our narcissistic preoccupation with getting ahead has prevented us from understanding the gospel call to self-crucifixion! We are taught by popular television preachers that we can be all we desire at a minimal cost to ourselves. So when God comes to us in search of servants, we slip quietly out the side door.

I have tried so often to reconstruct the scene in the upper room the night that Christ was betrayed. No servant was present to perform the customary washing of guests' feet. Jesus, waiting in vain for someone to play the role of a servant, finally takes the basin and towel, and washes the others' feet. There is clearly the strain of embarrassment in the room as he submits to servanthood.

Deep within, our narcissism makes us want to be served rather than serve. We think our search for meaning will inevitably end in comfort as others serve us. But we are too shallow to hold the riches of true joy. Viktor Frankl and Carl Jung agreed that the only answer to meaninglessness is to quit looking for meaning and to take up the mantle of service.

Even after we come to believe that Jesus Christ must be served, we still face the hurdle of dealing with our inadequacies. "God overestimates my abilities," we think. "He simply expects too much. I cannot measure up."

A Rejoicing Servanthood

In Luke 10 Jesus sends out thirty-five teams of ministers, all with the simple instruction to care for those in need and declare the kingdom of God. When they returned from their tour of ministry, their lives were marked with joy (Lk 10:17). I suspect it was not the kind of joy that one often finds in the church today. Rather it was the joy that goes hand in hand with ministry.

The first reason for their joy was that they had obeyed their Lord in the face of their fears. They must have been intimidated by the thought of going out as "nonclergy" to preach without Christ at their side. How could they equal the miracles and teaching of Jesus? But they did.

It is always scary to present Christ to our neighbors and friends and to face possible rejection and abuse. But this fear is always overcome by the joy that comes when we have taken the first, crucial step of obedience.

Another reason for their joy was that they had actually been trusted by Jesus despite their fears. I believe that eighty per cent of all Christians never know joy because they have never had to trust Christ. Usually we only attempt to do what we know we can do. So we never have one reason to trust Christ. We also never have true joy because we only accomplish what we can accomplish on our own.

How foolish we are to rebel against God's call to service because we think we can't handle some ministry. We forget that God never asks us to handle it by ourselves. He wants us to develop a dependency on his power. He calls us to do what requires trust to accomplish. But let us remember that the reward of utter trust is utter joy.

These thirty-five teams of witnesses had joy because they had seen God work. *God is never more than a philosophy until we see him act.* Most of us serve a God we have never seen do one victorious thing. But life acquires special meaning when we see God use us to do the unbelievable.

I am constantly involved in personal evangelism because I need to experience God acting through my life to touch others with grace. When God acts, therefore, I must listen. But even more I am transported by seeing his power at work in me doing what is neither ordinary nor explainable. This wonder is mine: the great Change Agent is changing his world through ministry and has used me as *his* minister!

God is here! God is acting! He is changing emptiness to abundance. Poverty to riches. Psychosis to sound thinking. Bereavement to belonging. Despair to delight.

Once we begin to perceive God acting, then like the seventy disciples we ourselves will be filled with a joy that will be as great as what we see recorded in Luke 10:17. But we must obey in the face of our fears, for only then can we behold the God who acts.

Let us no longer romantically glory only in the Jesus we worship, but let us go into the world with the Christ who commands, unafraid to serve as he requires. Then, like the seventy, we too shall return with rejoicing.

Notes

Chapter 2: Love by Covenant
[1]C. S. Lewis, "Cross-Examination," *God in the Dock,* ed. Walter Hooper (Grand Rapids, Mich.: Eerdmans, 1970), p. 261.

Chapter 4: The Mastery of Circumstance
[1]Francis Schaeffer, *Death in the City* (Downers Grove, Ill.: InterVarsity Press, 1969), p. 132.

Chapter 5: The Dynamic Mind
[1]Paul Tournier, *The Whole Person in a Broken World,* trans. John and Helen Doberstein (New York: Harper & Row, 1964), p. 12.

Chapter 6: Loving God
[1]Pieter Geyl as quoted in Martin Marty, *A Cry of Absence,* San Francisco: Harper & Row, 1983), pp. 17-18.

Chapter 7: Loving Our Mates
[1]Dorothy L. Sayers, *Are Women Human?* (Grand Rapids, Mich.: Eerdmans, 1979), pp. 18-19.
[2]William Shakespeare, *The Taming of the Shrew,* Act V, ii, 144-89.
[3]C. S. Lewis, *Letters to an American Lady* (Grand Rapids, Mich.: Eerdmans, 1967), p. 19.
[4]Paul Tournier, *To Understand Each Other,* trans. John S. Gilmour (Richmond, Va.: John Knox Press, 1968), p. 43.
[5]C. S. Lewis, *The Screwtape Letters* (New York: Macmillan, 1968), p. 17.
[6]Paul Tournier, *The Whole Person,* p. 89.